SHEPPTON: THE MYTH, MIRACLE & MUSIC

MAXIM W. FUREK

Sheppton: The Myth, Miracle & Music

Copyright © 2015 by Maxim W. Furek

All rights reserved. No part of this book may be reproduced or transmitted in any form or by any means without written permission from the author.

United States Copyright Office
1-2149845421 TXu 1-955-797

ISBN-13: 9781519145987
ISBN-10: 1519145985
Cover design by Danielle Crockett

Printed by CreateSpace
North Charleston, SC 29406

Copyright information follows for the lyrics quoted in this volume and are gratefully acknowledged.

"The Mines of Avondale." Author unknown. Variant of a Native American ballad, "The Avondale Mine Disaster" [Laws G-6] Native American Balladry (G. Malcolm Laws, 1950/1964).

Collected in 1951 from John M. Curtis of Trepassey, NL, and published in MacEdward Leach And The Songs Of Atlantic Canada © 2004 Memorial University of Newfoundland Folklore and Language Archive (MUNFLA).

MacEdward Leach also collected a variant published as #106, The Mines Of Avondale, in Folk Ballads And Songs Of The Lower Labrador Coast by the National Museum of Canada (Ottawa, 1965) Crown Copyrights Reserved. A variant was collected in 1956 from Charlie Weeks of Glace Bay, Nova Scotia, and published as #60, Mines Of Avondale in Ballads And Sea Songs Of Newfoundland by Elisabeth Bristol Greenleaf and Grace Yarrow Mansfield (Folklore Associates, Hatboro, PA, 1968).

"Sixteen Tons," written by Merle Travis. Copyright 1946 by Merle's Girls Music; Unichappell Music Inc. (BMI). All rights reserved.

"Timothy," written by Rupert Holmes. Copyright 1971 by Jordan-Herman-Holmes Publishing Inc., and Universal Music Corporation (ASCAP). All rights reserved.

On being entombed in the pit …

"The blackness of darkness which envelops the victim, the terrific oppression of lungs, the stifling fumes from the damp earth, unite with the ghastly considerations that we are beyond the remotest confines of hope, and that such is the allotted portion of *the dead*, to carry into the human heart a degree of appalling awe and horror not to be tolerated – never to be conceived."

Narrative of A. Gordon Pym of Nantucket
By Edgar Allan Poe.

Tolstoy remembered by his son…

"I know that I shall die soon and my mind is reconciled to it; but when I think that my body will be put into a coffin, that the lid of the coffin will be screwed down and I will be buried under the earth, I am horrified. I am well aware that my horror is unreasonable, that I shall not be feeling anything by then, but I cannot overcome this feeling."

Alexander Sergeyevich Buturlin, 1915, quoted by Sergei Tolstoy.

DEDICATION

This book is dedicated to those brave miners who risked their lives as they dug the Anthracite coal that fueled the Industrial Revolution.

TABLE OF CONTENTS

Acknowledgments		xi
Introduction		xv
Prologue		xvii
Chapter 1	Sheppton	1
Chapter 2	The Cave In	23
Chapter 3	The Ordeal	35
Chapter 4	Entombed	45
Chapter 5	Apocalypse	53
Chapter 6	The Beast	63
Chapter 7	Extrication	73
Chapter 8	Parallel Universe	82
Chapter 9	The Unspeakable	92
Chapter 10	Timothy	106
Chapter 11	Sheppton Mythology	120
Chapter 12	Village Pariah	136
Chapter 13	Hollow Earth	144
Chapter 14	The Good Pope	156
Chapter 15	The Technology	168
Chapter 16	Epilogue	175
Chapter 17	The Timeline	180
References		191
About the author		197

ACKNOWLEDGMENTS

This book took countless hours of research and writing to bring this project to fruition. I am indebted to the collective memories and recollections of the following individuals to whom I am most appreciative and grateful. Without them this project would have withered on the vine. Their story was recreated in their own words and from their vivid recollections. Their horrific experience was revisited and reconstructed by psychologists and psychiatrists who specialize in the area of confinement, entombment and trauma. We learned of the personalities of Bova, Fellin, and Throne by those who knew them, family members, acquaintances and some who spoke freely, but in complete anonymity.

Thanks to all who helped weave the Coal Region tapestry into a single cloth by sharing their valuable insights: George Andrews, John Bova, David Davis, Becky A. Farley, James Goode, Rick Hueholt, Kent Jackson, Steven Laychock, Steve Linn, Aveline Stees, Laurie McCants, Kelly Monitz, L.A. Tarone, Bill Trousdale, Van Wagner,

Art Whitaker, Steve Varonka, Troy A. Wolfgang, Dr. Peter Yasenchak and Carol Zielinski.

On matters of the psychological, supernatural and the unexplained I would like to thank John Baird, John Beers, Deena Budd, Rodney M. Cluff, Ed Conrad, Joseph Curran, Roland Gensel, Hank Houston, John Jones, Robert Marko, Robert McGee, Andrew Slembarski and Bob Whelan for their individual perceptions.

And to so many organizations who willingly shared their expertise, wisdom and encouragement that has allowed this project to go forward. Our gratitude goes out to the Anthracite & Industrial Minerals Mine Safety Division, Anthracite Heritage Museum, Berwick Historic Society, Bloomsburg Theatre Ensemble, Center for Western and Cowboy Poetry, Historical Society of Pennsylvania, The Historical Society of Schuylkill County, National Mining Academy, Pennsylvania Museum of Music and Broadcast History, United States Department of Labor Mine Safety & Health Administration, The United States Mines Rescue Association, and Wyoming Historical and Geological Society.

Thanks to Department of Environmental Protection Bureau of Deep Mine Safety for their comprehensive information on the "Sheppton Mine Disaster." Special acknowledgment to the United States Department of the Interior Bureau of Mines, District A for sharing with me their comprehensive and detailed "Final Report of Collapse of Slope Pillar Accident and Rescue of Two of the

Three Entombed Men, Oneida No. 2 Slope, Fellin Mining Company, Oneida, Schuylkill County, Pennsylvania. (August 13, 1963.)

And finally, many thanks to Chuck Werlie for reviewing my manuscript, to my wife, Patricia, for her love and encouragement, and to Dr. Ted Billy for his keen eye, extensive vocabulary and uplifting support of this project.

INTRODUCTION

The Sheppton saga unfolded in a deliberate measured cadence after three human beings became trapped hundreds of feet underground. It is a story of improbable rescue and pronouncements of the miraculous. It is a true story of human struggle that defies skeptics and nonbelievers.

The Sheppton Mythology (original title) was written as a result of my fascination for Schuylkill County and affinity for the unique Coal Region culture, immersed in mining lore and superstition.

In researching this book, news journalist and talk show host L.A. Tarone offered some sage advice as to timing. Tarone said, "It's too bad you're starting this now. The reporter who broke the story and who was on scene several times during the ordeal just died. Paul Cerula was a very good friend of mine and quite a mentor to me. I had tremendous respect for him and learned a lot from him. His reports about (Sheppton) were carried nationally on NBC radio. He knew everything about it and would have definitely talked to you about what he saw and what he knew.

He told me a lot of what happened, both on and off record. Paul was there on the early morning they pulled them out of that pit. In fact, his final TV appearance was on my show on WYLN several years ago and I indeed asked him about Sheppton."

Although I was unable to interview Paul Cerula, I did discuss Sheppton with countless others who helped fill in the blanks. Several individuals agreed to reveal personal stories and shared secrets, but only if their names were keep in strict confidence and NOT published! They spoke guardedly of a corrupt mining industry, harsh treatment of the miners and aspects of the bizarre and supernatural.

Much of our Sheppton recollection lives on through the words of Dave Fellin. Because of extensive documentation, notarized letters, thousands of printed words, televised interviews, and several books, we know of his experience. Fellin proved to be leader, spokesman and capable storyteller. Much of this book is told in his words and through his eyes.

He had strengths and faults, a mortal being challenged beyond limits, and an unlikely hero.

Despite the diverse elements of a mining disaster, murmurings of miracles and the supernatural and ugly allegations of cannibalism, I strived to piece together this strange convergence of variables in a logical and seamless manner. That was my mission.

I leave it to you, the reader, to decide if this has been accomplished.

PROLOGUE

Weird lights dance in the skies. People go missing. Unnamed creatures ambulate across desolate stretches of culm banks and things go bumpity bump in the night.

Walled in isolation, the Coal Region is a place of mystery and superstition. Averted eyes blink in silence. Unexplained nighttime occurrences are acknowledged in guarded tones while certain topics are simply ignored, pushed deeper into a shared repressed consciousness.

Although Centralia, Pennsylvania, is located some 20 crooked miles from Sheppton, one could argue that it lies directly at the intersection leading to the Gates of Hell. Centralia sits atop an underground inferno of smoldering anthracite. The demon fire is slowly, painfully, incinerating the town. The concealed coal seam has burned under this tiny community for more than 50 years, and has been the theme of countless books, horror films and documentaries.

According to legend, the town has been cursed. After being attacked and beaten by a mob of Molly Maguires (a secret society best known for their activism amongst Irish American miners in Pennsylvania's anthracite fields, and a group that some believe never existed), Father Daniel Ignatius McDermott, pastor of Centralia's first Roman Catholic Church, is said to have put a spell on the village, prophesizing that "one day St. Ignatius Church will be the only building standing in Centralia."

In 1992, Pennsylvania exercised the Commonwealth's eminent domain powers and appropriated the town. Essentially, the residents were bought out. The majority of inhabitants agreed to the government program that successfully purged the village of its human presence. But not all. Upon receiving an eviction notice, a retired miner shot his wife, then drove south of town and set himself on fire in his car. The curse persisted. Today Centralia is a weed-strewn ghost town where fewer than ten citizens reside, all breathing intolerable fumes of carbon monoxide and toxic gasses. Hidden fires burn beneath the streets, feeding on crisscrossed veins of anthracite coal. Vent pipes, jutting up like Whack-A-Mole heads, seem to be everywhere, spewing smoke and toxic gases from the raging subterranean blaze.

In nearby Carbon County, another Molly haunts the old Jim Thorpe jail. The ancient two-story lockup has a prisoner's macabre handprint outlined on the wall of prison cell 17. The inmate, Alexander Campbell, vowed that the handprint would forever remain on the wall as proof of his innocence. On June 21, 1877, "The Day of the Rope," four

Mollies, including Campbell, were hanged on the gallows for murder. Historians believe that the condemned men, seven in total, were falsely accused.

A complex Shakespearian play, Sheppton's curtain rose dramatically as it produced a second and then, an all-important third act. Fellin and Thrones' miraculous rescue captivated worldwide audiences, acknowledged by media outlets as one of the most important events of the year.

Everything about this occurrence was bizarre, unorthodox and inexplicable. Although the disaster took place in the small Oneida patch, it has always been attributed to Sheppton. Additionally, the Oneida #2 Slope was a non-union operation, known as a "wildcat mine." Due to its small size it easily circumvented safety rules and regulations of the day, creating the proverbial "recipe for disaster," and a further controversy.

After their rescue, the miners' story did not end. The most intriguing act unfolded when they walked safely on the top of solid ground, disclosing mysterious secrets experienced deep in that black tomb.

At the epicenter of the fabled Coal Region, Sheppton, steeped in the miraculous, the supernatural and the dreadful, has become greater than the sum of its parts, a modern day mystery and mythology that has yet to be unraveled.

Chapter 1
SHEPPTON

In the twilight days of 1963, Sheppton, a small village in the anthracite Coal Region, commanded the world's attention. During an implausible two-week period, this relatively unknown Pennsylvania patch town was gripped in a supernatural spell seeming to have neither beginning nor end.

Tiny patch towns like Sheppton sprouted up around the mining operations. They were a lacework of desolate wooden structures that seemed to have been constructed by a minimalist contractor. These company-owned communities, replete with company stores, held to the idea that the poor miner would never be able to work his way out of debt. Long hard hours, shoveling coal into a mine car or picking through slag defined their existence. They were paid according to what they mined. The harder they worked, the more they potentially could make. All was predicated upon one's ability to tolerate the physical punishment and trust the mining company's honesty. Neither was guaranteed.

Twelve-miles to the north, on winding Route 924, was Hazleton, the city closest to Sheppton. Hazleton was the ideal destination for shopping, socializing and opportunities to taste further aspects of blue-collar culture. Ann's Café on East Mine Street was a favorite hangout where Hank Throne listened to the Seeburg Jukebox and hillbilly fare like Marty Robbins' "Ruby Ann," Buck Owens' "Act Naturally," and Johnny Cash's "Ring of Fire.

Throne's buddies were Coalminer Dave Fellin and Louis Bova. Fellin was from Sheppton, further down the road. Fellin was often seen hanging around Dado's Bar on the corner of East Pine and Shepp Streets, about two blocks from his home. Louis Bova would occasionally stop in. Bova was an ardent dart shooter, expertly toeing the line, taking aim and hitting the bull's eye.

The Trio

Bova, Fellin and Throne are the subjects of our story. The trio of miners were working class guys, hardened and callused beyond their years. They were similar yet diverse. Fellin's father emigrated from the South Tyrol region, between Italy and Austria. Bova was also of Italian descent. Throne of German heritage. They were popular, described as being "mild mannered" and having lots of friends in the area. They were regular Joes with aches and pains, practical jokes and disdain for politicians and intrusive government regulations. The price of coal was always discussed, but more pressing matters were on their mind. Everyone complained about the Phillies who, even with Tony Taylor, Johnny Callison and Dick Allen, languished in fourth place and everyone talked about the Great Train Robbery after a gang of 15-armed robbers escaped with $7 million. At the time, it was the largest heist in Great Britain's history.

Stocky David Fellin was co-owner and operator of the Fellin Coal Company. Louis Bova and the younger Henry Throne were his laborers. Fellin, 58, stood 5' 8" and weighed 180 pounds. Married for 19 years to the former Anna Hoystrich, Fellin had four sisters, one brother and a stepson, Joseph Klein. The Sheppton resident referred to himself as "a hard-headed miner." He had explored and worked the mines since he was 15. That was who he was. That was all he knew. Dave had the gift. He was the schemer, the dreamer, the organizer, described as being "highly intelligent" and "sharp as a tack." Fellin was the one who could figure out a way to make a buck in a hard-luck patch.

Pattersonville's Louis Bova, 56, was the second oldest. He was also the smallest of the three miners. Because he stood at 5' 4" and weighed only 120 pounds, his physical stature was later be scrutinized in what was to become Sheppton's sordid mythology of rumor and innuendo.

He was married to the former Eva Kase and they had an eight-month old son. Bova had three sisters and five brothers, one of whom, Peter, had been trapped in a mine for seven days. Mine cave-ins were an unfortunate part of their family history; fear always a part of the equation, acknowledged more by some and less by others. Bova was scared. He often told Eva about the "creaking" sounds that the timbers made. It was as though the mine was secretly warning him about the mountains of coal threatening to unleash an angry avalanche of destruction.

Bova worked the graveyard shift, but after the birth of his son, he asked Fellin if he could be switched to days. Bova was a proud father and he wanted to spend more time with his son. The gleam in baby Johnny's eyes reflected heaven's light. Embracing the opportunity of fatherhood, Bova was in awe of his new role as "Dad." He was already dreaming about the day when he would let Johnny pick out his first bright red bicycle and teach him to ride. In many ways Bova was merely continuing the tradition and everyday rhythms established by his father and grandfather. And as his life immediately changed --- his sleeping patterns, the crying, Eva's maternal instincts --- he knew intuitively that this was the best thing that had ever happened to him. Yes, Louis Bova was a fortunate man.

Working hard to provide for his family he still yearned for more. He didn't want Johnny to work the mines and come home stinking and hurting and angry with his lot in life. Hopefully his son could do something else, perhaps land a job where he would wear a suit and tie and make good money with his mind, not his back. He wanted his son to leave Pattersonville and the mines.

Henry "Hank" Throne was the youngest of the group. In his 28th year he became a coal miner. Throne, although new to the mining trade, was a fast learner. He sported a well-trimmed mustache, and seemed to be forever smoking or chomping on a nasty smelling stogie. Throne had a certain swagger about him, a youthful air of confidence. Throne and his girlfriend managed Ann's Café at 30 East Mine Street in Hazleton and lived upstairs in a small apartment. Throne was a fan of hillbilly music and Sammy and the Valiants, one of his favorites, were regulars at Ann's Cafe. Situated next to grimy railroad tracks, the café would vibrate whenever locomotives and coal cars rumbled past, often when The Valiants would be playing one of their rockabilly tunes.

The trio filled their days with a grueling routine of work, sleep and dreams of a better life, hoping to replace this dreadful existence with a less dangerous and less physical profession. As July ran to its end and shadows lengthened, life went on, unsurprisingly, a day at a time. Coalminers Bova, Fellin, and Throne, were about to experience the horror that every miner dreads --- the horror of being entombed underground.

"Hidden Stream"

Despite its geographical location, Sheppton shared in the spirit of every other shadowy patch town. Sheppton could have easily been transplanted to the coalfields of Kentucky or West Virginia. Hard work and survival had earned it that right. And also legacy. Anthracite coal history began in 1790 in Pottsville, Pennsylvania, with the discovery of coal made by the hunter Necho Allen. It was in an area that became known as the Coal Region. According to legend, Allen fell asleep at the base of Broad Mountain and woke to the sight of a large fire after his campfire had ignited an outcropping of anthracite coal. By 1795, an anthracite-fired iron furnace had been built on the Schuylkill River and a thriving industry was being created.

With an elevation of 1,640 feet and a land area of less than 0.1 square miles, tiny Sheppton is tucked against the rural mountains of Schuylkill County in East Union Township. Schuylkill sits in the northeastern part of Pennsylvania, surrounded by the once rich anthracite fields that claimed the northern part of the county. The area takes its name from the Schuylkill River, the "hidden stream" accidentally discovered by Dutch settlers.

Northern Schuylkill County, where Sheppton is located, is due north of Broad Mountain. The region is predominately Catholic, Democratic and poor. During the United States presidential election of 1960, residents of Sheppton played a symbolic, yet key role. The charismatic Senator John F. Kennedy, a Catholic, carried Schuylkill County by 242 votes over incumbent Vice-President Richard Nixon, despite a registration margin of 65,540 to 37,592 that the GOP held over Democrats. The total census for the county was 173,027. Schuylkill helped Kennedy win Pennsylvania by a slim margin of 2.32%.

Kennedy, a ferocious campaigner, was elected with a lead of 112,827 votes, or 0.17% of the popular vote, giving him a victory of 303 to 219 in the Electoral College --- the closest since 1916. Moreover, Kennedy had the advantage of 17 million more registered Democrats than Republicans. Additionally, the Kennedy – Nixon election was the first time that all 50 of the current United States participated after Hawaii and Alaska became states in 1959.

Strange Time Warp

1963 languished within a strange time warp, a twilight zone contrasting equal measures of innocence and sexuality. It was three-years after the approval and marketing of Enovid, an oral contraceptive birth control pill that provided a reversible method of birth control and the beginning of the sexual revolution. M*ondo Cane*, the Italian shock-exploitation documentary, played in the steamy drive-in theatres that circled Sheppton. There were others, too, pictures with crazy titles like *The Girl Hunters*, *Cool Hollywood*, *Irma la Douce*, and the requisite allocation of nonsense, *The Day of the Triffids and King Kong vs. Godzilla*.

These were heady times. Sheppton residents watched as Soviet cosmonaut Valentina Vladimirovna Tereshkova became the first woman in space and James Meredith the first African-American to graduate from the University of

Mississippi. They also heard Rev. Dr. Martin Luther King Jr. deliver his "I Have a Dream" speech before a crowd of over 200,000 individuals gathered at the Lincoln Memorial in Washington, D.C. The year of '63 also saw hope dashed after race riots in Detroit and Birmingham bloodied the streets of America. The assassination of President John F. Kennedy played out against the ominous backdrop of Vietnamese Buddhist monks, who, in the most extreme form of self-sacrifice, doused themselves in gasoline before striking a solidarity match head.

Angry Mountain of Coal

Sheppton was a mining town and mining was a dangerous profession, cloaked within a violent and corrupt industry. It was unnatural to be working underground, almost non-human. The miners toiled in hazardous working conditions prone to mine cave-ins, explosions, flooding, toxic gasses and human error. All this coupled with the constant and obsessive fear that the mine ceiling could, at any time, without warning, come crashing down, crushing them to death, or, even worse, sparing their lives mercifully until their food, water and precious air dissipated as they gasped their last breath and slowly closed their eyes.

It was hazardous work. Despite countless safety regulations and precautions, shortcuts were often taken to assure a good day of production. That was the way of the mines. Dangerous. Unpredictable. They were human cogs in an inhuman machine, ground up human flesh sacrificed by the industrial machine called "modern America."

News traveled fast. Everyone knew when something bad happened. Church bells and fire sirens screamed out, penetrating the tiny patch town. A sickening feeling, resonating like a biblical plague, covered the entire community.

Everyone in the small patch towns heard stories or knew some poor soul who had died in the mines. Some friend, some neighbor, some family member who went underground and never returned. Some were crushed to death and others just went missing. Death was always close at hand, never far removed from the frigid depths of the mine tunnels. It was a predictable part of the life of the Pennsylvania coal miner, a life of hard work and suffering.

The omnipresent specter of death assumed many faces. Van Wagner, who found work in one of Pennsylvania's last deep anthracite mines, almost lost his life beneath an angry mountain of coal. Wagner recalled: "During my first week in the mine, I was entering the chute through the bottom manway and began walking on top of the loose coal towards the face or the working section of the mine. As I tried to walk on the loose coal, it began to shift like quick sand. More coal came down in sheets like an avalanche as I struggled. Before I knew it, I was buried up to my neck in coal. I have heard of several miners dying in this manner and wasn't in the mood to join them yet. I found that if I moved very slowly I was able to free one arm and slowly dig the rest of my body out without bringing more coal on top of me. The key to walking on loose coal is to keep moving your feet at all times. Lesson learned."

Many died for their trade. They were the workers, unskilled, uneducated, destitute, who came to America to experience the promise of streets paved in gold and the right to celebrate religious and personal freedoms, free from punishment. That pursuit of freedom permitted them to crawl like dogs into the dank coalmines, risking their lives as they extracted the anthracite that fueled the Industrial Revolution and made kings of the coal barons. They were actors in a black and white film. They lived off the land, not planting, logging or farming, but crawling underground, digging through the seventh circle of hell, to harvest chunks of black diamonds. They acknowledged their curse as a mixed blessing, a deal with the devil. In exchange for a livelihood that supported countless families, there would be a blood sacrifice for some unfortunate victim.

Disease, too. The doctors later called it pneumoconiosis, but in the patches they called it something else. Black lung was the genetic code that defined each miner's day and many an obituary. Every miner had it or knew someone who had it or died from it. It was the Coal Region's form of cancer, caused by inhaling fine coal dust particles over an extended period of time. Black lung killed slowly with unconstrained spasms that scraped mercilessly against one's throat. It made life miserable for entire families, kept awake by the wretched sleeplessness and coughing.

Their suffering was of no concern to the mining kingpins. In fact, as late as the 1960s, despite an increasing death toll from miner's lung disease, coal companies and incompetent governmental agencies denied the existence of black lung. Many company doctors absurdly testified that inhalation of coal dust made a miner immune to tuberculosis. Finally, The Coal Act of 1969 provided compensation for miners who were totally and permanently disabled by black lung, a small reimbursement for their ongoing suffering.

Bootleg Coalmines

The era of the independent bootleg coalmines sprang up in the 1950s after the larger companies opted to abandon underground operations and switch to surface mining. They accomplished this with huge dragline shovels, capable of ripping enormous amounts of coal and rock from the ground. Initially it was more expensive but, less dangerous. The miners did not have to crawl down into the earth, risking their lives, to dig out the veins of black gold.

Nonetheless, these abandoned mines provided an opportunity for the bootleg outfits. Usually under- regulated, the independent companies were able to mine the lucrative pillars of coal that had been left standing to support the ponderous roof of the mine. It did not always work out for the bootleggers. Often, after chipping away at the pillar, the collapsing pillar caused the mine to cave in on the ill-fated miners.

Geologically, the largest and most concentrated anthracite deposit in the world was located in Northeastern Pennsylvania, commonly referred to as the Coal Region. The deposit of "black gold" contained 480 square miles of coal-bearing rock and originally held an astounding 22.8 billion short tons of anthracite. (A short ton is a unit of mass equal to 2,000 pounds or 907.18474 kg). The Coal Region is roughly 100 miles in length and 30 miles in width.

Coal was King. In nearby Wyoming Valley, one hundred million tons were extracted from the earth, production peaking around 1917. But then the once-lucrative industry began to change. "Contract mining" companies, such as the Knox Coal Company, began to dominate the anthracite industry, replacing the larger corporations. The proliferation of the "contract mining" companies helped to increase anthracite tonnage post-World War II, but at what cost? Many of these newer operations would operate with old mining equipment and would often sidestep poorly enforced safety regulations.

Those cost savings efforts proved to be ill advised and, for some, fatal. It was the proverbial cost of doing business. Money begat power, access and influence. Dirty money. Hush money. Walking around money. Money spent to make law officials look the other way. There was plenty of money in the coal business, and it easily found ways to get into somebody's open pocket.

The road leading to The Kingdom of Coal was constructed, not of pretty yellow bricks, but of crunchy and malleable anthracite silt that molded easily to jack-booted feet, burning for endless hours. Miners worked long and hard, usually eight-hour shifts, pushing beyond human endurance. The work left them miserable, depleted and filthy. Coal particles became imbedded under leather-like skin, a type of coal miners' tattoo that conveyed a personal story of struggle and hardship. It was an authentic tattoo, not a contrived, superficial fashion statement of oriental letters and dragons.

Bova, Fellin and Throne. Their world co-existed in a parallel universe of tragedy and sad songs. Lamenting wives waited for their men --- filthy, starved, reeking of the stench of the underground --- to return. And 300 miles to the north, from protected, bannistered, widow's walks, wives looked down upon churning waters, praying for their fishermen's and sailors' safe return from the sea. The songs had comparable themes. Some sang about shipwrecks and others about terrible cave-ins.

All were soulful songs evoking the anguish of suffering families and communities. They mourned ill-fated coal miners, cursed to live their lives underground like human moles, and to die horrible fates: "The Mines of Avondale," intoned, *One hundred and ten of brave men were smothered underground / They're in their graves 'til the last day / their widows may bewail / And the orphans' cries, they rend the skies / all 'round through Avondale.*

And indeed the orphans' cries did rend the skies on September 6, 1869, where 110 men and boys died in Plymouth, Pennsylvania's Avondale Mine Disaster after a fire broke out, trapping the miners. A fire destroyed the coal breaker, located directly above the mineshaft. The shaft was the only entrance and exit from the mines. As the fire raged above, deadly carbon monoxide gas flowed into the mine. Despite the miners' best efforts to conserve fresh air, all 108 lives were lost. During rescue attempts, two brave men were overcome by gases and perished. The disaster resulted in America's single worst loss of life in an anthracite mine. That tragic accident brought about more stringent safety regulations. In 1870 the Pennsylvania General Assembly enacted legislation designed to enforce greater safety in the industry but also warned that, "All too often, mine owners ignored those precautions in the rush to maximize profits. This pressure grew worse with each passing decade as coal steadily lost its market share and prices plunged. By the middle of the 20th century, anthracite mining had lost its nineteenth-century boom aura, settling into a culture of corruption."

It was a pervasive corruption that traded profits for lives. In Pennsylvania, the mining industry saturated the land with a toxic chemistry of political, economic and social sludge. In return was the promise that hard work would lead to a better life and a brighter future.

That, too, was a lie as the miners were no better off than indentured servants, Caucasian slaves living in company homes, purchasing goods in the company store and never able to fully pay off their debt to the company. "Sixteen Tons," a song first recorded in 1946, and, later, covered by artists such as Tennessee Ernie Ford, Frankie Laine and Jimmy Dean, revealed a bitter truth:

You load sixteen tons / what do ya get / Another day older and deeper in debt / Saint Peter don't you call me 'cause I can't go / I owe my soul to the company store

The Knox Mine Murders

Sheppton was not the only place to bear witness to the suffering and grief. The death knell of ringing church bells echoed throughout the anthracite fields of Pennsylvania, sometimes ignored, sometimes accepted, as an occupational hazard. The forewarning had previously been scrawled on the wall some four years earlier. The tragic and senseless Knox Coal Mine Disaster struck on January 22, 1959. Twelve miners were entombed; their bodies swept away and never found, the consequence of a dangerous, poorly regulated industry.

The Knox Coal Company, operating in an atmosphere of avarice and corruption, forged a cartel between greedy company and union bosses. They ruled in this era of anthracite. The blood of 12 innocent men stained their hands, the result of selfish, wanton actions.

At around 11:30 AM on January 22, 1959, the Susquehanna River broke throughout the thin rock roof of the River

Slope Mine, operated by the Knox Coal Company. Estimated at 150-feet in diameter, the whirlpool-like hole sucked in ten million gallons of water and ice "like a bathtub drain," flooding miles of interconnected mines throughout the Wyoming Valley. Thirty-three miners would eventually escape. The bodies of the 12 remaining workers were never found.

By the afternoon, plans to seal the breach were already in effect. One of the railroad tracks above the cave in was cut and bent towards the river. A staggering amount of materials were then pushed into the whirlpool by a powerful locomotive in an attempt to stop up the hole. More than 50 Hopper cars, 400 mining cars, thousands of bales of hay, hundreds of railroad ties, and tons of culm, dirt and rock were thrown into the watery hole.

Nothing worked.

The angry Susquehanna could not be stopped.

In a final attempt to block up the hole, the river was diverted at two points around Wintermoot Island as two separate dams were constructed. After pumping out the water, tons of rock and clay were poured into the gaping hole and a solid cap of concrete was poured in the opening.

Officials of the Knox Coal Company and its lessor, the Pennsylvania Coal Company, the owners of the River Slope Mine, had ignored clearly marked "Stop Lines" on their maps. These "Stop Lines" determined where mining could not take place because of inadequate roof thickness. Although state law prohibited mining within 35 feet of a riverbed, the River Slope Mine was a mere 19 inches from the Susquehanna. The companies continued to mine off course, and well out under the Susquehanna River. There was less than two-feet of protective rock and gravel that separated the miners from the pressure of ten billion gallons of dark, icy water.

According to historian Chris Murley's faithful account, "They then pumped much of the water out of the mine to look for the twelve missing miners. No bodies were ever recovered. How could this tragedy have happened? The original plan was to keep fifty-feet of rock and coal between the workings and the river bottom. The Knox Company wanted this to be lowered to 35 feet. Mine inspectors deemed this okay, as it would be sufficient to stand up to the river. At this point the seam of coal sloped up towards the river in what is known as an anticline. Company owners kept pushing the miners closer and closer to the river bottom until the rock could no longer support the river. At the point where the river broke through the rock was only five to six feet thick!"

According to *ExplorePAhistory.com*, "The mine had been illegally excavated beneath the Susquehanna River at the direction of the Knox Coal Company. When the force of the ice-laden river broke the thin layer of rock, over ten billion gallons of water flowed through this and other mines. This disaster ended deep mining in much of the Wyoming Valley.

"The Knox Mine Disaster also exposed the corrupt tactics of United Mine Workers officials, mine management and mafia-connected interests in the mid-20th century. A grand jury investigating the cave in found seven men guilty of involuntary manslaughter and three of them also guilt of conspiracy. All the convictions, however, were overturned on appeal. Without justice then, it is little wonder that a daughter of one of the drowned miners called the disaster, the 'Knox Mine Murders.'"

The disaster at Knox ended most deep mining in the Wyoming Valley and signaled the end of the "boom" days for the region. In the aftermath of the Knox Disaster, and later, the Sheppton Disaster, the mining industry began to die a measured death. The statistical snapshot of the mining industry in Pennsylvania was depressed and disconcerting. In 20 years, anthracite tonnage dropped from 60 million a year to 16 ½ million a year. The Commonwealth of Pennsylvania, once the nation's mighty locomotive, was painfully grinding to a halt.

Finding individuals willing to work in the mines was beginning to prove difficult. On Friday, August 9, 1963, the Glen Alden Coal Company purchased ads in Wilkes-Barre and Schuylkill County-area papers announcing employment opportunities. The U.S. Armed Forces in Europe had placed a 710,224-ton order that was to be divided among six coal companies. "Why the shortage of coal miners?" the article asked. "An industry spokesman said young men are refusing to work in the mines, and older men aren't being replaced." It was called "out migration," and the coal region would watch as their young men began to leave the patches and company homes for the cities. They refused to work in the mines as their fathers had. It was a different time, a different era. Even the downtrodden immigrants now had choices and opportunities. Mining coal was not high on their list.

After World War II, the era of King Coal was ending. The coal industry had a tawdry reputation of danger and corruption. Wealthy coal barons, in buttoned-down collars and pretentious top hats, raped the land and then walked away. Like an infectious cancer, ugly hills and mounds of slag dotted the mountains. Once-clear streams now were blackened with mining toxins and industrial pollutants. Left behind were desecrated mountains where only opportunistic white birch trees could take root and blossom. Mining left more permanent destructive than the "slash and burn" technique, a primitive method of cutting and burning forests to create fields for agriculture or pasture for livestock. This was the dirty legacy that the coal barons left for future generations, a legacy that still haunts us today.

The search for more cost-effective and cleaner fuels made coal a poor choice in an era of environmental awareness and political correctness. Other energy sources such as oil and natural gas began to win favor with the masses in each successive decade. After another deadly mining episode occurred on their watch, the mining industry became even more regulated and restrictive. On March 1, 1977, the Porter Tunnel Mine in Schuylkill Countys' Tower City led to the deaths of nine miners. With no chance for escape, they suffered an unfathomable death as their mine chamber was flooded by inrushing water that had entered the mine through a breach in the mine floor, turning it into a dark watery grave.

Oneida #2 Slope

With each death, the day of the independent, bootleg mining operation was coming to an end. As the mines began closing, the employment opportunities disappeared, one by one. All that was left – collieries, strip mines, slag heaps and culm banks - were the remnants of the early days when King Coal ruled and transformed places like Sheppton and Oneida into thriving Boomtowns.

The Fellin Coal Company was a small outfit operated as a partnership between Eugene J. Gibbons of West Hazleton and David Fellin. The entrepreneurs owned the Oneida No. 2 Slope, one of the few remaining independent operations in the region.

The Oneida No. 2 Slope, dormant for years, had not been worked regularly since August 1956. A temporary "abandonment notice" was recorded on March 25, 1957, but, two-years later, co-owner Gibbons performed rehabilitation work, including retimbering along part of the slope. Because of increased demands for anthracite, the mine was reopened.

Gibbons and Fellin thought that the mine was safe and up to standards, but, more importantly, they believed the mine was a potential moneymaker. The average daily coal production at the Fellin Mine location was about 15 tons, and approximately one thousand tons of anthracite had been produced since the mine had reopened.

That productivity was a boon for many of the workers, and one of the few opportunities that they had. The Oneida No. 2 Slope provided a steady income and livelihood for Fellin and his workers Bova and Throne. It was arduous work, at times, pushing them beyond human capacity, yet it gave their families sustenance and the means for survival in a most difficult time.

Oneida's single-entry mine used three and four-man crews for the operation. Three men toiled underground with one on the surface during the day. During the graveyard shift, two men worked underground and one remained on the surface. These smaller bootleg operations, usually with a crew of five or fewer workers, operated under the radar.

Because such crews were not subject to the restrictive safety regulations laid down by federal and state officials, they were unfortunately the sites of numerous accidents. The incident at Sheppton would become one of them. The miners' most difficult ordeal, only moments away, began at the start of a typical work shift. Louis Bova, Dave Fellin and Hank Throne were about to suffer a torment few men will ever realize, and experience a living nightmare that would haunt them, mercilessly, for their remaining days.

Chapter 2
THE CAVE IN

It happened on a Tuesday.

The morning began as usual. Shortly before 7:00 a.m., the underground crew of Dave Fellin, Hank Throne and Louis Bova descended into the mine.

After reaching his workstation, Fellin, the mine foreman, inspected the slope. He indicated that work was about to begin. The men and equipment were in place, ready for another workday and another continued ritual with the emphasis on safety and teamwork. The specific duties to be performed by the work crew consisted of making necessary tests and safety examinations, installation and inspection of roof supports, loading loose material into the slope buggy and any other work necessitated by the slope-restoration project. Those chores were ritualistically completed in another well-rehearsed act of déjà vu.

Sometime after 8:00 a.m., a pile of loose coal was shoveled into the ancient buggy, a ritual that would be repeated throughout the work shift again and again.

After those tasks were completed, the buggy was loaded and topped off. The rusted slope buggy was the most valuable part of the operation. The buggy, like a prehistoric creature, would be filled, shovel after shovel, with its valuable treasure. Fellin visually checked the slope and signaled an "all clear." The time was approximately 8:50 a.m. Fellin and Throne retreated to their shelter area, west of the slope. Bova moved to the signaling station on the east side and signaled Walker to send down the buggy by pressing the buzzer several times.

The loaded buggy, its wheels struggling, ascended the track about 40 feet and reached a point just above the east shaker gangway. The buggy's wheels were pulled via thick cables against iron rails. It reached the top and tipped its cargo as Walker then reversed the process. He sent the buggy down for another load.

On this day George Walker had a gut feeling. He knew something bad was about to happen. Walker watched the buggy dump its load and begin the return trip down into the mine. Without warning Walker's prophetic horror of horrors, that miner's sixth sense, rendered an ordinary workday into a surreal nightmare. In the blink of an eye, the hoisting cable snapped like an elastic band. A portion of the east-slope supporting pillar, located above the shaker conveyor gangway, collapsed as the mine buggy jack-knifed off the track. The ponderous slope buggy, huge and reptilian, tumbled like a bomb, 300 feet into the depths. It ripped out wooden beams supporting the mine roof and careened down into the shaft.

No human should have to experience the horrible sound of that cataclysmic roar. It was as though someone had detonated a nuclear bomb. The shockwave knocked Fellin sideways, sending him rolling against the floor. The sound was deafening, and he felt a sharp pain in his ears. Ear-shattering sounds exploded against eardrums, concentrated and magnified by the elongated span of the mineshaft. Part sound, part vibration, it was terrible and audacious in its magnitude. The deafening shrill scream of the slope buggy suddenly morphed into a monotonous thrumming that threatened his sanity.

Like bowling balls hurled by a madman, tons of rock and coal flew at the miners. The ceiling of the mine chamber collapsed with an explosive sensory assault. Structural timbers, beams designed to keep the men safe, fell down like flimsy toothpicks, filling the slope for almost seventy feet above the miners.

The escape route leading to the top was blocked with tons of debris. There was no other way out. The miners were trapped.

In an immeasurable moment in time they were smashed to the ground, separated from their loved ones by a mountain of rock and coal. Throne thought the three were lucky not to have been crushed to death. He would never forget the exact moment when his world turned upside down, stripping away any sense of reality. He later recollected, "Louis rapped three times for the buggy to go up and dumped the coal. Coming down, it got only half way down. That's when the big rumble started. And all hell broke loose. The timbers on the wall next to us caved in and the timbers on the ceiling above us came down. We just managed to step aside in time as the big chunks of wood and coal and stone fell wildly around us."

Fellin later described that awful event "as similar to a wooden matchbox being crushed." It happened so fast he was incapable of any sane comprehension. There was no measure, no barometer to gage or to understand. It was the essence of victimization, of being totally upended and trapped, of having despair choke out all trace of hope. He straddled a line between the familiar and the unfamiliar, entering a place where all things known had died, buried in soil consecrated by the devil himself.

Fellin's body ached. His eyes couldn't see through the particles of dirt and rock. As his helmet bounced back violently, his forehead slammed into something hard. The air was clogged with dirt and coal dust. He attempted two dry gasps of air but only sucked in tiny daggers of coal. He probed a finger along the inside of the miner's helmet searching for something bad, touching his cheek and face, checking for blood.

He felt like a mad scientist's experiment gone wrong. After the first cave-in, the events that transpired were predictable. Tons of rock and coal began to shift. In an act of savage homeostasis, the rushing mass of rock and coal sought to quickly fill every vulnerable empty space. Here, the laws of gravity and physical science applied.

Throne recollected that after the initial cave-in "there were five or six others (cave-ins) which forced us to try to find a safe place." Throne remembered those moments, right after the disaster: "In the first hour and a half, we just sat there against the wall while the debris piled higher before us in the tunnel. The rumbling from the cave-in lasted that long. There were others later," Throne said.

At the time of the cave-in, Throne and Fellin were on one side of the railway tracks, Bova on the other. With the exception of one time when the two were able to communicate with Bova, they lost all contact with their mate. They yelled his name and he responded. His voice sounded small and wounded. Bova said that his leg had been broken during the cave-in. He was in extreme pain. That was the last time Fellin and Throne spoke with their companion. They would never hear Louis Bova's voice again.

In an Associated Press interview, Throne said, "We could see Louis on the other side until the power line to our work lights broke. For the next couple of hours we could see a little around us with the lights on our helmets. But then they burned out. Our matches wouldn't burn down there. That was the end of the light for the next five and a half days," he said.

After the overhead lights feeding off the power lines were severed, the mineshaft was thrown into almost total darkness. Light and vision were slowly extinguished, but, as a further punishment, they were blinded by a vortex of swirling coal particles. Their battered miner's helmets cast illumination that barely cut through the falling curtain of dirt and coal dust. The beam reflected weakly against the walls. The lamp became fainter by each minute; ghostly shadows, flickering as the lights died in irregular spasms, left the miners in unimaginable dimness. Perhaps total blindness would have been preferable in that harsh and unforgiving crypt.

The walls were collapsing all around him, showering him with shards of coal. He fought panic. Fellin's recollection of that moment was seared into his brain. It was always there. It would never go away. "Suddenly everything was coming down – timber, coal rocks. We could see it because the power line was still working. The stuff was rushing down between us and Louis. Then it was quiet for maybe half a minute. Then the rush started again. It went on like this, starting and stopping for some time. I was trying as hard as I could to concentrate, to listen, to judge how much of the shaft was being filled by the cave-in. I figured it filled up about 75 feet from the bottom."

They sat in shock and horror but not in silence. The rushes of the cave-ins continued for days upon days. The earth would give them no peace; would not release them from their claustrophobic terror.

Buried Alive

For a miner, there was no greater terror than the threat of being buried alive. Trapped underground with little chance for rescue is a concept too horrible for the mind to comprehend. It is a consideration capable of driving men insane. The closed in space, the lack of fresh air, the claustrophobic feelings of walls crushing in tighter and tighter and the realization of a hoped-for rescue that was not to come. These were all part of the panic that held them in an icy grip.

But Fellin was an experienced hard-headed miner. He used his brain and not his gut. He knew that survival was all about time and presence. It was not about the future or past but about now, about being in the moment. It came to him in a dream or in a REM state, like a hallucinatory tidal whisper. As best as he had it figured, they had to get through a minute and then another and five more minutes and then an hour and then a day and another. Maybe then, after that passage of time, they would be rescued from the subterranean prison. He tried to stay positive and chase the demons away.

That was a hard thing to do. Hank said something that Fellin kept thinking about. He asked, *What if we ran out of air and died from lack of oxygen?* Hank wasn't far from the truth. It could happen. Easily. Even now they were choking on polluted air unfit for human beings, more suited for Martians or alien creatures. Fellin's lips were parched and dry, his tongue tasting like a slag pile of colliery waste. *Maybe Hank was right. Maybe they were dying!* Hank Throne's pessimism, like a country song, sought to become the dominant chords. Fellin fought to shut out the serenade of that evil, hell-spawned music.

Trapped

Every time they descended into the mine, they cast the dice of death and glory. Peter Bova, brother of Louis, knew that feeling. He often told the men how he faced the reality of dying in the mine. He prayed to God to make it through this horror, praying day after day. He also knew the frustration when hope runs out and the harsh chill of reality sets in. "I know," Bova told a reporter, " I spent seven days trapped in just such a mine – seven days and seven nights in 1948 when I was in the mines. Every minute seemed like a day. It doesn't affect your mind. There is no fear of the dark or being closed in. A miner is used to that. His life is always being closed in on. His life is in the mines, so the mines hold no terrors. But the knowledge that you're trapped, that you will die – that is the terror. You just think and pray... and keep praying."

Both Fellin and Throne heard stories of miners who had died. The cemeteries of Schuylkill County were dotted with memorials and worn crosses to those whose remains would never be discovered or claimed, the victims remembered by special masses and prayer vigils and families coming together to revere the names of those brave souls who had been lost to the mines.

They would be remembered as miners who sacrificed it all for their families' security and the mining company's profit.

Hope Fades

Shortly after their arrival at the disaster scene, State Secretary of Mines Dr. H. Beecher Charmbury and Deputy Secretary Gordon E. Smith of the Pennsylvania Department of Mines and Mineral Industries met with co-owner Eugene J. Gibbons. The state officials were informed that the Fellin Coal Company had no funds for any proposed rescue operation.

An immediate assessment had to be made. It appeared that the three miners were hopelessly entombed in the dank bowels of the earth. The trio were sealed in a silent anthracite catacomb, trapped 300 feet under tons of tightly compressed rock and coal. There was little hope for them.

That sad observation had to be communicated to the families of the trapped miners. On the day after the cave-in, Charmbury visited two of the families of the trapped miners. He described hopes of finding the men alive as very "dim." He said if the men weren't killed by the cave-in, there was a chance they could have died of suffocation. The *Hazleton Standard Speaker* headline screamed out: "Fear 3 Area Men Killed in Sheppton Mine." The *Pottsville Republican's* headline read, "Hope Fades For Three Miners in Gas Filled Sheppton Pit."

Faith died as despair settled in. Co-owner Gibbons lamented, "There was little hope they could have survived the rush of coal and rock, or the saturation of the slope with deadly black damp." Deputy Attorney General Leon

Herlich proposed a petition asking the Schuylkill County Court to hear testimony to determine whether the men could realistically be saved. The question of a possible rescue attempt became more of a business decision in which allocations of time, energy and available monies are reviewed by a rapacious Board of Directors, concerned only with the bottom line.

There was little optimism or promise on that tragic August day. With the momentous amount of debris that had pulverized and clogged the mine's shaft, all appeared stark and discouraging. Tons of debris, including huge chunks of timber, lay in the path of the rescue workers. Those same tons of debris, many believed, had crushed and buried the miners in a ghastly underground grave.

"Anyone who looked down that slope after the cave-in would not believe that anyone could have survived," Andy Drebitko, the miner later christened "Mr. X," stated. "They were ready to seal it and declare them dead," author Ronnie Sando explained of the initial inspection of the clogged mine shaft. And even Dave Fellin's brother, Joe, emotionally concluded, "There is little hope for my brother and the others."

A collective pessimism led to the final option, one whispered in shamed and hushed voices. That cold-blooded possibility was to bulldoze and level the entire Oneida slope area and then encase it with protective concrete. It would be a final shrine to the three entombed men.

This likelihood was perhaps the lowest ebb; the nadir of despair, after all possibility of hope had been abandoned. That ghoulish circumstance had been visited upon the Coal Region before. *The New York Times* reported in an article (May 30, 1924) titled "VETERAN BURIED BY MINE CAVE," an account of Isaac Rough, Civil War veteran and miner. Rough, along with 14 others, died in a cave-in at the Stockton Mine. Rough was buried 400 feet underground, his body never found. The article explained, "Eventually the cave-in was filled up and a marble marker placed on the restored levels of the earth. The monument was enclosed by a fence, trees were planted and today the little plot is in the midst of a village almost deserted, because the Stockton mines have been worked out for years and all but the top level of the workings are filled with water."

Death was a frequent visitor to the Coal Region. The church and grief-stricken community knew full well what was next to come.

Due to the physical absence of the miner's bodies, St. Joseph's Catholic Church would view the Sheppton incident as a "special circumstance." First, the Funeral Liturgy would be celebrated with the sorrowful congregation. Next, the Rite of Committal, the last of the Funeral Rites, would be commemorated. The rituals would be performed, sadly, near the mine's bleak entrance.

Because of widespread media attention additional music and readings, a brief homily, and petitions would also be included for the mourners. Then the good people of

Sheppton would dedicate their special shrine to the entombed miners and have Father Sverchak offer a final prayer in memory of the dearly departed Louis Bova, David Fellin and Henry Throne.

Chapter 3
THE ORDEAL

Crawling on worn hands and useless legs, Fellin and Throne survived in an alien milieu of total darkness. Their knees ached, their nostrils, clogged with dirt and coal particles, burned. They sucked in coal dust and coughed themselves to sleep. Soft mounds of coal-glazed silt crunched beneath their feet as they searched for a way out, calling for Louis Bova.

They found neither.

For the entombed men, there existed no barometer by which to gauge the passage of time. Absolute darkness, perhaps the worst of circumstances, greeted them. Like a surreal Renaissance painting, each August day melted into an August night, and, in an endless series of repetitive and maddening turns, it continued that pattern again and again. Dust particles, like dandelion seeds, danced in the air. They spun against the dim light of the helmets.

The light in the battery-powered lanterns lasted for several more hours. After that, even the lifesaving waterproof matches were spent, useless. There was no illumination. No electric or gas or florescent lighting. The remaining light, dim radiant numerals, reflected from a solitary luminous dial. Eventually, even that sliver of hope, provided by a studied glance at the wrist, would eventually stop glowing, in a final mockery of their senses.

The ordeal was worst for the young and inexperienced Hank Throne. The 28-year-old had nothing to compare this to, no recollection of anything like this in his youthful memory, and now --- the unspeakable darkness that met his wide opened eyes. For the first few hours Hank Throne had been able to gauge the passage of time from the faint glow of his florescent wristwatch. That worked for a short period. Then, he became confused as to the hours and days. Now, it had become darker. Morning and night blended into a morass of something indefinable, something that had no limits and shared the exact sameness.

It was getting worse. Already cursed with blindness, Throne's hearing now became an excruciating chamber of horrors. After the initial cave-in, the persistent ringing never dissipated. Throne's eardrums vibrated. A horrible hum tortured his ears like a Gregorian chant. He had no feeling. No sensation other than the dull throbbing of his teeth, that had been smashed by the onrushing debris. The fear had sucked out everything. Throne had departed his body. He was left with nothing --- sick with sadness, defeat, and emptiness. He was overwhelmed by torment and fear, but, slowly, his emotions dissipated like melting snow, clogged lungs forcing breathing to a slowed measure. He recognized a long peal of church bells and a choir singing hymns of celebration. They were sweet and hopeful, yet foreboding. He yearned for rescue, but knew, in his heart, he was already in the grave.

Symbiotic Relationship

Throne had developed a symbiotic relationship with the older miner, perceiving him as mentor and father figure. Throne's only hope came from the controlled articulation of Dave Fellin, instructing him in philosophy, mining safety and ways to avoid danger. Fellin listened to Throne's fears with empathy and compassion. He listened. He heard.

Another intangible quality that Fellin possessed was something of the religious and of the spiritual. Fellin spoke enthusiastically of President Kennedy, the first Roman Catholic to be elected President. As Senator, John F. Kennedy challenged students to give two years of their lives to help people in developing countries. Because of his appeal, many young people from Schuylkill County joined the Peace Corps and, with a renewed sense of volunteerism, offered to serve their country.

Fellin's zeal was contagious. John XXIII, the Good Pope, was exciting the masses by calling for change. John wanted to modernize the church and talk with Marxists and Communists. Although not a religious person, Throne liked hearing these things and began to share Fellin's sense of church, community, and belonging.

331 Feet Below

The miners languished in a claustrophobic tomb, encased within a cloak of rock and coal, a coffin-like opening that held neither light nor warmth. Again and again they called Bova's name. An eerie silence was the sorrowful response. Trapped 331 feet beneath the surface of the earth, Fellin and Throne lived with the chilly possibility that they had already died.

They were always exhausted, their muscles sore and hurting. The chamber was littered with fallen timbers. Fellin and Throne propped them up against the chamber roof to protect themselves from any further collapse.

With lifeless bodies stuffed in a dreadfully confined space, the roofline so low that the miners were unable to stand erect, they crawled like beasts. Hoping against all odds to find a way out, they pressed on. It was like a crack addict, crawling on the floor, searching for the phantom rock, wishing it to magically appear. Fellin and Throne's road to survival traveled through the gates of Hell. The duo endured the possibility of hypothermia, dehydration, claustrophobia and madness. It was the worst way to die, slowly, painfully, lacking in any comfort or promise.

Until that point they had endured countless days, devoid of light, food and potable water. What they would give for a long sip of cold, sparkling water. On average, adults lose about ten cups of fluid a day --- in urine, feces, perspiration, and exhaled breath. Fluid needs to be replaced by drinking water, while the remainder is obtained from solid food. They tried to suck moisture from the timbers used to prop up the roof. They later discovered a small stream running through the mine. In yet another moment of torment, they were forced to drink from a brackish and pungent pool of muddy sulfur water.

Throne sensed the strange beast. It stirred. It had slumbered for centuries and now assumed the form of stark, primeval fear. The shadow stalked them in silence. Their fear turned into deadening paralysis. It was called "miner's psychosis," when the walls of reality were crushed in a vice grip of numbing terror.

Throne spoke about his bleakest moment, when he was pushed to his limit. He could calculate the exact instant when the taste of bile lodged in his throat and his body convulsed into spasms. Filled with sulfur water, pieces of dried out timber beams and dirt-coal particles, his belly threatened to burst. He wanted to vomit but couldn't. It would have been easier to choke to death than to puke his guts out. Throne was bloated and numbed. He wasn't hungry. Any hunger pangs had disappeared into yesterday, like Bob Wills' "Faded Love." They had listened to that song hundreds of times at Dado's. Wills and his Texas Playboys had recorded it and right now it played over and over and Throne couldn't get it out of his head. It oddly kept him from losing his mind.

Fellin felt he was going to die and later reflected on those horrible days of entombment. He said, "I thought we might be finished... the fifth day was when I began to think they had forgotten about us. When I thought someone had let me down, I felt worse. I couldn't hear the drill and I thought we should have been out by then. I think that was the closest we came to death. That's when it started raining and we could hear it coming down the drainage pipes and we thought we'd be drowned. Thank God it rained only twenty minutes."

Those 20 excruciating minutes forced them to remember an earlier incident, one they would have been better to purge from their memories.

Four years before, in 1959, the Knox Mine Disaster screamed out a horrific warning about the dangers of mining. Throne had read about Knox in the Hazleton papers. The Susquehanna River flooded the mines and drowned 12 hapless miners. The mine had been transformed into a watery grave. Blaming the mining company, someone called the tragedy "the Knox Mine Murders." Everyone at Dado's talked about it, mourning the fate of his fallen brothers. Stanley "Stosh" Kuzminsky said they "drowned like rats."

Knox was the nail in the coffin.

It ended the mining industry in the upriver Wyoming Valley, leaving only small, sparsely regulated independent operations to bring out the coal. Fellin contemplated that negativity. He forced himself to purge Knox from his consciousness. He had to control his thoughts or otherwise would gnash his teeth and go stark raving mad. There could be no thoughts of the dark horror that was his existence. Henry Miller wrote, *"For madmen never cease to dream that they are dreaming."*

Fellin was forced to cast all negative thoughts aside and transcend that consciousness. He had to find a reason to survive, something to focus on, a mission that went beyond mere survival. Rats did that ---survive. He was better than a rat. He was a man of faith. *Let me walk with you, Jesus.* But still, his faith was not enough. He needed good works down in this private hole of darkness. Maybe he could protect Throne. That would be his mission. He had little else. Visions of the past swirled. The past few years had moved fast. After leaving the farm in Zions Grove, Dave and Anna relocated to Sheppton. Fellin had been working the mines for 43 long years, since he was 15-years-old. The entrance to the Oneida mine slope was literally in his back yard. But that was now only a sweet memory.

The mine cold as a tomb. Mine temperatures remained constant due to moisture and the insulation of tons of rock and coal deposits. A bone numbing 50-degrees made their struggle for survival a life-threatening endeavor. The miners, their skin cold and numb with grayish-yellow patches, faced the gruesome possibility of frostbite. If body temperatures dropped below 95 degrees Fahrenheit, hypothermia could set in, leading to confusion, uncontrollable shivering and lowered core body temperature. These conditions, plus stress and dehydration, often lead to unconsciousness and death.

Throne was scared. He was shivering. He felt his core temperature dropping. Shivering was an automatic thing, a physiological attempt to raise his body temperature and give him another shot at living. He clenched his teeth and tried to stop them from chattering.

They did what they could to stay alive in that pit. Thorne later recounted his ordeal, how they hoped and prayed and held each other until the shaking turned to a peaceful numbing sensation. Throne just wanted to stay alive: "To keep warm, I'd sit with my legs spread and David would sit between my legs with his back to me and I'd breathe on his back and neck. All the time we'd be rocking back and forth, also to keep warm. Then David would switch and do the same for me. We'd do this for five to ten minutes at a time. Then we'd stop but only for five minutes, say, because then we'd be cold again. Most times it felt like about 30 degrees above zero."

Even thick coveralls and thermal undershirts offered little protection from the constant, demanding cold. Both said it was so numbing that they "couldn't think straight." They were never able to get comfortable, never able to find warmth or comfort. This was not the place for that. The constant chill took refuge, creeping into their bones. Unable to find warmth, their muscles tightened and cramped. That horrible complaint was killing them … slowly. It was a curious tradeoff --- swapping the hot sun and intolerable heat outside the mine for an unendurable bone-chilling numbness. They kept each other alive, their respective body temperatures providing warmth. Said Fellin, "To keep warm, we'd sleep face to face with our arms around each other. We'd sleep maybe half an hour and then the cold would wake us and we'd start rocking again to get some circulation."

Being entombed gave Fellin lots of time to think. Immediately after the cave-in he felt an explosion of crippling pain, his head bursting. He heard somebody screaming. He thought he had been killed and then crazy, insane hallucinations covered him like snakeskin. His flesh crawled. His heart sickened. He sensed their enclosure was tight, enveloping, a dystopian horror. Would they live to savor a final gasp of air, and last a moment longer? Fellin began to panic. He reached out for Hank Throne.

He realized that he had better manage his thoughts and think this thing through correctly. There were rules down here. Only the survivors were smart enough to adhere to them. He articulated slowly to himself, mouthing the words silently, so that Throne would not hear. Fellin was a man. He was not a lowly rat, crawling through mud and fecal matter. Stosh Kuzminsky was the self-appointed rat expert. A regular patron at Dado's Bar, Stosh's purpose in life was to impress others with anything memorized from his personal copy of the *Encyclopedia Britannica*. Stosh informed the crowd that male rats were called *bucks* and unmated females were *does*. He continued that pregnant or parent females were called *dams*, and infants were called *kittens* or *pups*. A group of rats is either referred to as a *pack* or a *mischief*. Stosh joked about the *mischief* one could face in the depths of the mineshaft.

Fellin refused to dwell upon the *mischief* or the obnoxious Kuzminsky. He was stronger than that, and more than a mere character in one of those heartbreak songs played on the Seeburg jukebox at Dado's Cafe. "500 Miles Away From Home." "The End of the World." "Still." "Six Days on the Road." Music wasn't about sound; it was about meaning and feeling. In a sense they were all the same, all revisiting themes of loneliness, longing and alienation.

Perfect songs for a guy trapped below the earth. He knew them all. Fellin had spent a small fortune playing those sad shit-kickin' songs and slamming down cold beers, one by one.

Right now he had to tune those lonely songs out from his head. He could not allow himself to go crazy. He had to take care of Hank Throne.

Chapter 4
ENTOMBED

Sheppton was a conspiracy of sorts, a horror show of bad luck and terrible karma that prevented an immediate rescue. An explosion of coal shrapnel rained down, ferociously, like blackbirds plunging from the sky. After the initial collapse, another series of cave-ins, ongoing, relentless, dropped with maddening frequency. The shaft was choked with debris. Deadly fumes of black damp gas made rescue impossible, and initial rescue plans estimated it would take 50 days to extricate the trapped miners.

Time was being wasted. It took precious time to locate and then transport specialized drilling bits and equipment to the remote disaster site. Rota-drill equipment was shipped down from Scranton and a Davey 6-inch rotary drill was dispatched from western Pennsylvania. Even after the drilling began, a violent electric storm forced the rescue team to cease all operations.

The rescue team had little hope, but finally, some good news arrived in a world that harbored none.

On Sunday August 18, just before high noon, the six-inch wide drill pierced through the chamber's roof. The crew had broken through the cave roof, but destroyed the drill bit in the process.

The curse that was Sheppton persisted.

It took another eternity to snake a microphone down the jagged and constricted borehole. The microphone plunged more than 300 feet into the silent depths of the labyrinth. The rescuers listened for signs of life. After all, that was the purpose of the mission --- to determine if Bova, Fellin and Throne were dead or astoundingly alive.

John Biros shouted down the borehole and heard a response. The miners were alive. Biros began to shout, "They are alive. I hear them. They're alive." The news reverberated throughout Sheppton like a rogue tsunami.

After six tedious days, the rescuers succeeded in reaching Fellin and Throne. They were alive and overjoyed. The borehole would be their lifeline to the surface, and precious human contact. "When the drill came through, it almost hit me on the head," Fellin recalled of the rescue attempt. He was ecstatic as the drill bit pierced through the roof of the cramped mine chamber. It was possibly the best moment of his life. Hours later a microphone was snaked down the borehole. Fellin grabbed it, and in a moment of bravado, shouted defiantly, "We're not afraid of anything down here."

In a final report from the U.S. Bureau of Mines, the moment when rescuers made contact was documented. The report impassively stated, "Fellin reported that he and Throne were uninjured and had found refuge on the west side of the slope, and that they had communicated orally with Bova, who was on the east side of the slope and had sustained a hip injury."

91.44 meters

They calculated that their restrictive enclosure was about fourteen feet long and nine feet wide. They couldn't be certain, and, in the end, nobody seemed to know. The exact specifications of Fellin and Throne's entombment would be calculated and studied by mining engineers and industry specialists. They were trapped more than 310 feet underground, about the length of a football field. The depth would be computed to be 91.44 meters.

But the actual size of their entombed space was an area of much dispute. The catacomb that imprisoned them for 14 cruel days was estimated to have been about ten feet in length and six feet in width. The roof of the chamber was low, and ranged from two and a half feet to six feet in height. The trapped miners had to crawl to get around as they desperately searched for a hidden passageway that would miraculously take them to safety and cool fresh air. There were some spaces where they could actually stand on two feet, a reminder that they were still human beings and not lowly animals.

A local newspaper reported from the site from the beginning and became an important source of information nationally. Hazleton's *Standard Speaker* described the coffin like space as being two feet wide by ten feet long, while a former staffer, Ed Conrad, said, "Fellin and Throne were trapped inside a chamber only about ten feet long and three feet wide, with a six-foot ceiling."

Life Magazine Photographer George Harvan described the confines of the tomb, and perceived it as "a very narrow place" and "a very confined space … being six foot long and perhaps four foot wide."

Maddening Circumstances

Some said it was a miracle that Fellin and Throne weren't crushed by the hundreds of tons of rock that poured down during the tremendous cave-in, robbing them of vision and hope. In hindsight, it was determined they were spared because of their precise location. Jumbled timbering materials, in a maddening game of Pick Up Sticks, prevented a small pocket, a monkey shaft west of the slope, from filling with debris materials. Debris from the cave-in, paradoxically, helped protect them, and, ironically, saved their lives.

In his book, *The Famous Sheppton Mine Rescue*, Ronnie Sando described the purpose of monkey shafts. Sando called them "little shafts set apart from the main shaft that they (the miners) would dig out to store their tools and supplies in and in the event of a cave-in, could run into it and use it for cover. This particular shaft was about 16 feet long and six feet wide, at the opening it was about six feet high and it went to 18 inches in the rear."

Throne felt the world shift under his feet. His was an unholy universe that taunted him, shaking him to the core. His feet seemed to drag. Despite protection by steel-toed boots, something was wrong. He wiggled his toes. No response.

Throne knew too that without food they would suffer temporary blindness, caused by lack of vitamin-A and lack of visual stimulation. Fellin had told him that. But what did that mean? He was already blind. There was no light. His eyes always stinging, eyesight scorched from millions of particles of dirt and coal that scraped against punished eyes.

Throne remembered the initial cave-in, the unexpected jolt that felt as though a massive iron fist had slammed him against the slope floor. Panic bulged in his chest, his ribcage aching. *Is this what it feels like when you are about to die?* Throne lay there for what seemed to be a long time. He thought his spine had been broken. He was afraid to move, afraid to learn that maybe it had been. His breathe jammed in his parched throat as he floated, drunkenly, in and out of consciousness. His stomach churned, and then, filled with caustic, unforgiving acid. He wanted it all to end.

Throne had only been working in the mines for a very short time and suddenly, at the age of 28, was swallowed by the earth. Throne was the youngest of the three. He had only been working with Fellin for two months but he had worked other mines in the past and had served a tour of duty with the U.S. Army. The miners used the word *entombment* like a profane curse. It was the most obscene word Throne had ever heard, conjuring up vile images. Now he knew exactly the meaning of that profanity.

Fear oozed ominously. It infected everyone and assumed countless faces. Water. Fire. Entombment. And rats. The rodents scurried in the slopes. Underfoot. Squeaking. The miners looked for rats. It meant the air was breathable. Rats shunned methane gas. And sensed mine vibrations. Some miners fed the rats to keep them around and to keep them safe. Even now, the two men were alive and breathing. There was still hope they could be located and rescued.

The rescue of Louis Bova was another matter. John Tancredi, Bova's lifelong friend and godfather of Bova's son, believed in the impossible odds. Tancredi said "around here we knew him as 'the demon of the woods.' He can survive anything." Tancredi explained how Bova would go hunting or fishing in the woods without a coat or jacket and brave the elements over several days. "He knows how to take care of himself," Tancredi said. "Unless the whole roof falls in on top of him I'd give odds that he's alive and will get out. He's the demon, and he has nine lives."

On their sixth day of entombment Fellin and Throne received soup, lights and medical supplies, sent down through the borehole. But Louis Bova was not so lucky. Assuming that he had survived the initial cave in, there is no proof that he had access to water. Boreholes were being driven into the ground in attempts to locate him. Hope was dwindling for the vanished miner even as Eva Bova, knowing the toughness of her man, held out for a miracle.

Peter Bova knew that the odds were not in favor of his brother. He candidly admitted to reporters, "My brother is going to die. I know it and he knows it. He's been a miner too long not to realize the shape he's in. The other men will get out, but after they pull them out, they'll have to drive a shaft underneath that section of the tunnel to get into the first tunnel.

"You can't work a rescue shaft into the other section. Maybe they'll try from the top, but whatever they do, it will be too late. Lou will starve to death by then. He's on borrowed time now."

David Fellin feared for Louis Bova but knew instinctively that he had to face his own anger and fear. He waged a private war that, if lost, would lead to self-sabotage. (It would be the end of them.) Psychologically, he was trapped between self-doubt and the slender hope that, somehow, they would be saved from this place of near-death. He had to remain focused and positive. He had to believe in himself.

Those were the thoughts of a coherent, cognitive David Fellin. In the Oneida No. 2 Slope, something inexplicable happened during Fellin and Throne's entombment. It happened slowly. Their long days of total darkness, numbing cold, and inability to savor joy or tranquility, virtually killed any higher consciousness. Their purpose was not to think or rationalize, but to endure. They were human beings, yes, but beings relegated to mere survival. Energies shifted from brain to heart, chest cavity rising, sensing loneliness and sadness. It was the cruelest hurt, not from the conscious mind, but from the aching heart --- the worst pain man will ever have to withstand.

Trapped desperately within that Stygian pit, Fellin and Throne were about to enter the realm of madness.

Chapter 5
APOCALYPSE

For Eva Bova and Anna Fellin it seemed like the end of the world, the Coal Region version of the apocalypse. They sat in lawn chairs praying for news that their men were alive and well. Or...that their bodies would be retrieved.

A regional newspaper reflected, "Although presumed dead by most people, the relatives cling to the faint hope the three may still be alive." It was a slim ray of hope, an implausible prospect, and a viewpoint not shared by the majority of villagers.

Quickly, the Sheppton mindset grew into one of utter despondency. Bova, Fellin and Throne had been entombed for five days. There was no communication with them. Electric signal lines had been severed during the cave-in. Tappings by the rescue crew went unanswered. Someone asked a state official about the trapped miners. There was a lack of enthusiasm in his response.

To reach the miners the rescue crew would have to drill through hundreds of feet of layers of rock, clay and hardened sand particles. It was impossible to reach the miners through the entrance shaft. That escape route had been blocked by the cave-in and was impassable, filed with tons of coal, rock and timber. But there was another consideration, too - to attempt a rescue through this entranceway could easily produce additional cave-ins and possibly lead to the death of the miners – if they were indeed still alive.

Although the Department had no legal authority for the expenditure of the funds, important decisions had to be made immediately. Three days after the cave-in, on August 15, a formal request was made for federal and state funding. The total for the rescue operations was estimated to be around $60,000. A legal investigation of the financial status of the Fellin Coal Company was ordered by the Department to proceed concurrently with the rescue operation. The legal investigation confirmed the financial statement of co-owner's Eugene J. Gibbons and David Fellin.

No funds were available in their account.

The rescue attempt almost didn't get off the ground. Initially, rescuers who had entered the shaft detected black damp, an odorless gas. Ventilator fans were installed to suck out the polluted air. By Wednesday morning officials believed that the deadly gas had been removed. Attempts were made to descend 150 feet and then 200 feet down the crawl ladder into the slope. The air appeared to be safe to breathe but now officials were concerned with the continuous rushes, aftershocks from the initial cave-in. The rushes continued for days, an indication that the mine's anger was not lessening. There could be no rescue attempt until the mine slope had stabilized.

State and federal mining officials had developed a risky plan. Because the entire area of the shaft entrance was dangerous and unpredictable, they would seal the shaft of the mine to prevent further cave-ins. Then, another borehole would be sunk in an attempt to reach the trapped men. But, that strategy, if agreed upon, could take up to 50 days, authorities estimated. That was too long to hope for the men's survival. A traditional rescue attempt was out of the question. Sheppton demanded an alternative strategy.

Joseph Fellin, brother of the trapped miner, had another idea. At his insistence, officials of the local district of the United Mine Workers Association agreed to attempt a rescue of sorts. Fellin convinced the UMWA to drill two boreholes. They would drill a six inch-wide borehole down to the mine chamber to determine if the miners were still alive. Some believed that if the miners had somehow survived the cave in, they were tucked within the safety of a monkey shaft. Officials said the only chance the men had to survive was to find an open area of the shaft not blocked by debris or filled with deadly black damp gas. Joseph was assigned the task of finding the spot where the drilling operation was to begin. It was an attempt at appeasing the family members of the trapped miners, as well as an opportunity to utilize the mining expertise of Joseph Fellin.

The drilling of the two boreholes began on Saturday night around 6:30 p.m.

While possible rescue plans were being devised, politics entered the picture when Lewis Evans created a huge controversy. Evans, the former Secretary of Mines and Mineral Industries, was now employed as a special representative to the United Mine Worker's Association. W.A. "Tony" Boyle, UMWA President, dispatched Evans to Sheppton and, on the fourth day of the cave-in, Evans visited the Sheppton site. In a statement issued by the UMWA, Evans specified that the attempt to find the miners was a "rescue operation" and not a "recovery operation." He wanted to make it clear that the UMWA intended to save lives.

After it was determined that at least two of the entombed miners were still alive, the method of rescue required action on the part of State Mines Secretary Charmbury and Deputy Secretary of Mines Gordon Smith to obtain equipment and supplies needed to perform the rescue operation. This was done "without any hesitation and with full knowledge of the financial status," according to official press releases, affirming that it "was the immediate actions of Charmbury and Smith that helped spearhead the rescue attempt."

What really happened behind the closed doors of the politically connected? Did the UMWA have to convince state officials to attempt a rescue operation, or did the UMWA use this situation as a means of promoting their own agenda and propaganda efforts? Which version was the more accurate? Some came closer to telling the truth than did others.

Military Operation

When the drill broke through to the trapped miners, a tremendous roar broke out among the hundreds of spectators and workers gathered at the location. The number of individuals was estimated to be around 500.

A mass of curious onlookers had converged upon the rescue site --- family members, dignitaries, teenagers, big-city reporters, and regular people hoping to witness a miracle. The Sheppton mine became an epicenter of excitement and optimism. Red Cross tents were erected. A city of small tents sprouted like mushrooms.

Commonwealth Telephone set up a communications tent with 39 telephone lines and phones for reporters to file their stories. More than 40,000 feet of cable was laid. Commonwealth draped new private (not multi-family party) phone lines along dusty haul roads. The Salvation Army drove in their red "chuck wagon" truck. Sammy Touch, leader of Sammy and the Valiants, even performed live at the rescue site, strumming his guitar and singing into the microphone. Touch and his band had played at Ann's Café and were one of Throne's favorite country bands.

Mine Secretary Charmbury held regular morning news conferences, detailing the progress of the operation, and keeping the situation on an optimistic note.

The perimeter enclosing the Oneida No. 2 Slope resembled a war zone replete with refugees and a disorderly social structure. Trees surrounding the cave-in looked dead, as though they had been baked in a massive oven. The rescue procedure grew into a military operation as Pennsylvania State Troopers and the National Guard cordoned off the perimeter, manning barricades and controlling frenetic crowds from wandering back to the Oneida No. 2 slope, which would hamper rescue operations. It was getting out of hand and turning into a mob scene. Order and the rule of law had to be quickly established. The A Company 165 Military Police Battalion was sent to Sheppton to suppress the crowds of frenzied spectators. Ironically, Henry Throne had been a member of this MP unit, prior to his bartending and mining ventures.

After six arduous days, the rescue attempt had succeeded in reaching them. Sadly, Louis Bova was not among them. After the two survivors were discovered, *The Associated Press* noted, "The drama of rescuing men trapped in mines is not new to the people who inhabit the regions where men dig for a living." The miners would now be forced to endure the second phase of the attempted rescue, but one that did not ensure certainty.

Hank Throne's brother, Andrew, celebrated the occasion. He somehow managed to hold on to dwindling slivers of hope, praying for the impossible. "It was a miracle. We were very anxious and scared wondering whether he'd ever come out, but we always thought there was a chance."

Andrew Throne echoed the sentiments of many of the faithful villagers.

Through that life-saving 6-inch-wide borehole, the trapped miners received food and drink and medication that reduced the swelling in their hands and feet. A microphone was sent down. The rescue team quickly established communications with Fellin and Throne, who helped the rescue team coordinate rescue efforts. Amplifiers allowed them to talk with their families.

A temporary hospital tent, manned by a U.S. Navy physician, was set up at the work site. The physician communicated with Fellin and Throne at regular intervals to determine their physical condition. Special medicinal ointments were lowered to the men.

Additional medical doctors instructed them in calisthenics to help circulation and range of motion abilities, as well as emotional well-being. It was an amazing, coordinated attempt to keep spirits and hopes alive... an attempt at resurrection. They even snaked down an electrical cord with a light bulb at the end. Now, at last, the trapped miners would have some light. Maybe they could find a way out – unless they were rescued first.

The Sheppton Miracle

What happened next can only be described as "The Sheppton Miracle." An army of friends and neighbors, rising up to meet the impossible challenge, began to amass around the Fellin Coal Company "contributing their time, talents and facilities." These hardened people had always expressed an unshakable faith and vitality. They represented the indomitable American spirit that rose up at the proverbial eleventh hour. The self-sufficiency and resiliency of the coal region, which went beyond mere survival, had always been there --- Sheppton only brought it into clearer focus.

An earlier account of the outpouring of support described the altruism that surrounded Sheppton: "Miners, who had worked an eight-hour day, came to the rescue scene and volunteered an additional four to twelve hours to help. Some helpers did not leave the scene, but ate and slept there to be on hand for all emergencies. Coal companies, drilling companies and other companies sent their most technically qualified officials free of charge to the scene to provide technical advice and help. Industrial companies from all over the country volunteered their equipment and supplies. Even schoolboys from the area helped to do many a job that had to be done. Government agencies of all types contributed ever so much to the rescue operation."

Salvation Army Food Bank

The omnipresent Salvation Army, under the direction of Major Donald Lance, 41, provided more than coffee for the workers. A regional newspaper documented the importance of the Salvation Army and the scope of the tremendous undertaking: "The monumental job of feeding the hundreds of personnel involved was capably handled by the Salvation Army. Two mobile canteens on the scene dispensed 4,000 gallons of coffee; 3,000 quarts of milk; 4,000 gallons of water; 400 gallons of soup; 600 cases of soda; 200 gallons of other cold drinks; 600 dozen doughnuts and other pastries; 16,000 sandwiches; 1,000 servings of ice cream; 75 cases of apples, oranges, cantaloupes, nectarines, peaches, plums and watermelons; plus incalculable amounts of candies, meatloaf, chicken, roast beef, fish, spaghetti and meatball dinners."

Authoritics later calculated that as many as 7,000 meals were served daily by an armada of staff and volunteer workers, enough to provide for the hundreds of individuals who gathered at the site.

An armada of officials, National Guard MP's and hordes of media hovered near the rescue site. Fr. Michael P. Sverchak, of St Joseph's Church, kept vigil and offered prayers with the townspeople.

Anna Fellin and Eva Bova maintained a constant vigil, awaiting any news of their imprisoned husbands. They sat near the rescue site on lawn chairs, exhausted, offering each other support and words of encouragement. Anna was often seen sitting between her son and her niece. Sometimes Eva's eight-month-old son Johnny would sit with her.

Much of the rescue effort came in the form of volunteer services. If all labor, professional services, equipment, supplies and other expenditures had to be paid for, it is estimated that the total cost of the rescue operation in 1963 dollars would be between $300,000 and $500,000.

The total expenditures, however, due to the outpouring of volunteer services and unsolicited materials amounted to an astounding $61,606.95.

On the 10th day of their entombment, Governor William Scranton visited the disaster site. It was August 22nd. In a letter published by the *Associated Press* Scranton stated: "I told them (the trapped miners) how proud of them everyone is. They brushed off their own courage as unimportant and praised the work of the rescue crews who've been working day and night to free them. They know all too well the predicament they're in. But they belong to a vanishing breed of men who've spent their lives mining anthracite coal. Such men are tough and courageous. They don't waste time feeling sorry for themselves."

Fellin certainly did not feel sorry for himself. That wasn't part of his "hard headed" agenda. Fellin was the acknowledged leader. Mining since the age of 15, he had 43 years of experience over Throne. Four decades of experience, information and possible strategies gave him an inner peace and confidence. Fellin was steady as a rock, and Hank Throne recognized that. Throne admired the effortless way that Fellin navigated through life. He admired the older man's maturity and confidence, acknowledged that Fellin possessed more character and resilience than he could ever dream of.

Throne would soon be tested, forced to mature beyond his years. Time was running out. He knew that his only chance of survival was by following Fellin's lead.

Chapter 6
THE BEAST

The attempted Sheppton rescue employed a fantastic secret weapon, something that might have been found trashed on a Hollywood science fiction backlot.

The Bucyrus-Erie 50-R was a 55-foot high behemoth that rose 11-stories tall and housed a massive drill. Weighing a staggering 65 tons, its gigantic derrick ascended defiantly into the sky, an American flag proudly waving atop the structure.

The 50-R was the perfect machine for the Sheppton rescue operation. The Beast was one of the most commanding machines in the world. Valued at $160,000, it was only one of two such apparati in the immediate area. Driven by 4,100 volts of electric current, provided by a tire-mounted diesel-powered 600-1,200 kilovolt mobile generating unit, the imposing machine was equipped with a 12-inch-diameter bit that would be changed to a wider size once the trapped miners had been reached.

The Beast required huge amounts of power to function efficiently. Another mechanical brute, a 12-cylinder D-1700 Caterpillar diesel engine was housed in a special trailer and generated enough power to keep the entire operation humming. The Cat had been located through the Correale Mining Company, a valuable Hazleton resource that was part of the statewide industrial mining network. Additionally, a number of diesel-powered mobile air compressors, positioned about 100 yards up the hill from the rescue site, were secured to provide an adequate supply of air for the drill units and to blast the drill shavings out of the borehole. That was to prevent an avalanche of drill shavings from blanketing and suffocating the men who were trapped below.

Other pieces of equipment included an Ingersoll-Rand Airflo compressor, with a capacity of 1,200 cubic feet per minute at one hundred-pounds per square inch, and another with a capacity of 900 cubic feet per minute.

To sufficiently ream the six-inch borehole, a drill bit had to be secured to widen the hole. None could be found in the immediate region, but, after numerous phone calls, an appropriate tip revealed that one was located in Houston, Texas. Billionaire Howard Hughes, owner of the Hughes Tool Company, had such a device. Drill extensions, described as Tungsten Carbide cutters, designed to fasten to a drill, were sent to Hazleton aboard a U.S. Navy plane. To facilitate the procedure, Hazleton-area workers designed and constructed ten hollow-steel sections. Each section measured 32 feet, nine-inches in length and was attached to the main shaft that would rotate the drill tip.

Three-part maneuver

One of the unsung heroes was Louis Pagnotti Sr., owner of the West Pittston-based Sullivan Trail Coal Company and the No. 1 Contracting Company. Pagnotti, a former mule driver, was a confident and generous individual. He was well liked and respected by his men, often described as being "fair" and "humble." Pagnotti supplied the 50-R drill, which, at the time, was being used on a highway construction project.

The epitome of altruism and benevolence, Pagnotti contributed men and equipment for the rescue attempt. Nine of his workers were part of the effort, with three crews of three working eight-hour shifts. On that note, Pagnotti rejected any issue of monetary compensation.

"We have no idea what it's going to cost. Nobody talks money. The only thing at stake is the men," he clarified of the monetary expenditure. As far as reimbursement from state or federal coffers," he explained, "We were never promised, nor we never asked."

"It isn't only me. Everyone does it. When you operate in a town and can do something good for the people, you do so. We're just praying we get the men out. That's the only interest we have. No one ever mentioned who is going to pay. No one ever asked. It isn't everyone who can do it because they don't have the equipment. It's a pleasure when you're able to do something," Pagnotti said of his participation.

The rescue attempt was to be orchestrated in a labor-intensive, three-part maneuver. Spaced 20-feet apart on the surface, two boreholes would be made. The initial six-inch borehole was attempted by a high speed, Rota-drill, supplied by Scranton's Sprague and Henwood Drilling Company. The hole was aimed toward the center of the mine slope, near the face. On Sunday, August 18, at 9:50 p.m., after boring 331 feet through the incredible mass of rock and coal at the Number One Hole, no sign of life was detected.

A Voice!

A similar procedure was tried at the Number Two Hole by using a Davey rotary drill. The truck-mounted drill, shipped in by the Pittsburgh-based William Glunt Drilling Company, began to drill at a site Fellin's brother, Joe, had recommended. Assistant Mine Foreman, Joe Fellin, had contacted the United Mine Worker's Union in Hazleton with his plan. The Davey drove a six-inch borehole over 300 feet into the site aimed to intercept the center of the east gangway, 15 feet from the slope rib. After breaking through the cavern, the rescuers shouted down. Through the metallic borehole they heard a muffled human voice calling back. It was the broken, yet ecstatic, voice of David Fellin, upon his sixth day of entombment.

It had taken 22 hours of drilling a six-inch borehole to reach the miners. Two appeared to be alive. Now, the second phase of the rescue operation depended on a more powerful machine --- the Bucyrus-Erie 50-R.

Superintendent Jimmy Gaughn, of the Sullivan Trail Coal Company, gave his workers strict orders. The 50-R had to be immediately disassembled and, after arriving in Sheppton, reassembled. Drilling was to begin the next day. Usually the arduous procedure took three days. Sheppton would be different --- for obvious reasons. Workers had to disassemble the 50-R drill, burning off the nuts and bolts with acetylene torches, and then, hopefully, reassemble the Beast at the Sheppton site. The Beast was loaded upon one of Pagnotti's rails, a flatbed trailer used in highway construction and large enough to support the massive weight of the electric 50-R drill. A convoy of Pennsylvania state troopers, back-up vehicles, utility trucks and the flatbed lumbered from the small mining community of Janesville through downtown Hazleton, south on Poplar Street and west on Broad Street to Route 924 and then another 10 miles to the Sheppton cave-in.

As it crawled along, creating traffic congestion and lines of spectators amazed at the size of the 50-R, the slow-moving rig snagged utility lines, pulling them down, as it proceeded. A fleet of utility truckers and linemen immediately replaced or reconnected the lines. It became more practical for some of the residents to temporarily lose power, than to stop the convoy and deal with the power lines.

Bone-numbing vibration

Turning south, the convoy moved onto Route #924, passing the Montfort Motel, and then entered the Village of Sheppton. Their unorthodox route was a geographical patchwork of busy blacktop that transformed into country road and then, magically dissolved into gravel.

In preparation for the Bucyrus-Erie Beast, bulldozers provided by Hazleton's Pindar Trucking Company cleared the area at the Sheppton site. They leveled out the rough areas and ridges. Piles of timbers were unloaded by massive dump trucks. Workers, choking on the tar-like creosote stench, cribbed the front of the 50-R with massive railroad ties, lugged and hand placed. Those timbers would form the sturdy foundation, the cribbing, for the colossus drill unit. It would have to be anchored firmly for the delicate rescue attempt.

The drill operator was 39-year-old Michael Rank, a resident of Bethel, Connecticut, recruited for the rescue attempt. Rank's machine had to be greased, bolts tightened and the drill head constantly checked. The drill had to operate smoothly and without snags. There were lives at stake. The powerful 50-R drill exerted up to 75,000 pounds of precise, focused pressure, the perfect device for the task at hand.

The entire area was cloaked in a bone-numbing vibration, a penetrating and insistent hum that reverberated down to one's core. It was loud and deafening, difficult to endure. Angry and unrelenting, the drill droned throughout the day and night. Sounds created by the generators, the trucks and the mighty Bucyrus-Erie beast, with its high-pitched whine, were deafening, but, even worse, was the piercing blast from the Caterpillar's exhaust. The workers had to get used to it. They had no other choice, and besides, they weren't the ones entombed 300 feet below.

The 50-R began rescue operations at exactly 3:40 a.m. on August 20th. It was a hot and sweaty summer night. The entire perimeter of the rescue site had a surreal feel to it, especially during the evening hours after the sun dipped below sleepy mountains surrounding the mine. Strings of light bulbs, gently swaying back and fourth, were strung around the perimeter allowing the rescue crews to go about their business of keeping the "Beast" working. Huge floodlights were positioned on spider-like light standards. The entire area, bathed in bright artificial light, illuminated the nighttime, allowing workers to labor around the clock, like colonies of army ants.

One-hundred-pound bags of Quick Gel, stacked in symmetrical piles, were poured into the hole as it was being drilled. The Quick Gel would seal any cracks in the rock, in the event that the drill struck water. The rescue team didn't want to flood the miner's chamber --- that would assure a slow and agonizing death.

The crew was working as quickly and as carefully as they could. The worst thing that could happen would be to break off a drill bit or snag into the rock formation. God forbid if they had to slow down the rescue attempt! That would be problematic. It would cost them valuable time. Already, the miners had been trapped underground for eight days. Even though they were sending down food, coffee and electricity to the entombed miners, time was running out.

Panama Canal

The Ohio-based Bucyrus International Inc. had a history of innovation and successful projects. They had been leaders in the industry for decades. Bucyrus had a history of designing and constructing machines when a project demanded something that was beyond the existing technology of the day. The largest American project for which Bucyrus' equipment was utilized was the project to enlarge the New York State Barge Canal from 1902-1912.

Another big project for Bucyrus machines was the construction of the Panama Canal. The project, which took place in 1904-1914, used 77 shovels to excavate 225 *million* cubic yards of earth. It was a huge undertaking, a project of grand magnitude. Many felt it would never be completed.

Bucyrus also contributed to the Chicago Drainage Canal, shipping 24 of the 171 steam shovels it built in production to the project

The former Bucyrus-Erie Company developed some of the largest and most powerful blast-hole drills in the industry. Their products were created in response to a need in the mining industry for drills capable of blasting through impenetrable rock formations. In 1946, Bucyrus developed the 42T, the first Bucyrus churn drill with hydraulic leveling jacks. The product line was successful beyond imagination. 11,600 churn drills were sold up to 1984, many of them still in worldwide use today.

Bucyrus had always been the master of innovation. In 1952. The company introduced the first commercially successful, large diameter rotary blast-hole drill. The rotary drill replaced the churn drill, which used a reciprocating action that raised and dropped the steel rod bit into the hole. With compressed air as a bailing agent, the 50-R was the first in a long line of R-series blast-hole drills, called "high-production drills." This was the machine used during the 1963 Sheppton rescue attempt.

Over the decades, the value of Bucyrus International Inc. had been demonstrated strikingly to the world. In November 2010, Caterpillar Inc. announced that it would buy Bucyrus International Inc. for $7.6 billion. Caterpillar, the world's largest maker of construction and mining equipment, found itself with $2.3 billion in cash reserves at the end of their third quarter. The acquisition of Bucyrus International Inc. allowed Caterpillar to add to its line of mining equipment, in high demand in emerging foreign markets. Despite its profitability, since 2000 Caterpillar has avoided paying $2.4 billion in U.S. taxes by shifting profits to a wholly controlled affiliate in Switzerland, this prompting a senate subcommittee hearing to investigate the matter.

The superior technology of the Bucyrus-Erie 50-R Beast is without question. It allowed a larger borehole to be drilled, rapidly, more than 300 feet, in a dramatic rescue effort. The method of rescue utilizing the 50-R was completely new. After the Sheppton incident it would be used in other parts of the world, saving countless lives.

But, the final question, still pondered and unanswered, remained. If the miners were rescued, who or what deserved the most credit for this?

Would we attribute the successful rescue to the 50-R Beast, or did Fellin and Throne's lust for basic human survival play a larger role? Did they have the will to endure the unendurable and beat the apparently unbeatable odds, or were they merely pawns in the game of modern technology and the 50-R?

Chapter 7
EXTRICATION

Everyone knew that the rescue attempt would be extremely dangerous. The original plan was to extricate the men with bullet-like capsules, lowered to the slope's bottom. The seven-and-a-half-foot cylinders, designed at Hazleton's Pagnotti Enterprises, would tightly enclose the miners and then be pulled to the top of the surface.

On August 27, at 12:20 a.m., the steel drill, prepping the way for the capsules, was pulled from the hole.

However, there was more bad news. Upon further inspection, the rescue team observed that the steel bit had lost a minimum of gauge and the lower five-foot section was irregular, causing several "knees" or ledges at the higher elevations in the hole. That was not the situation the team had expected to find. The borehole was not smooth and predictable, as hoped, but a dangerous maze of irregular crevices and protruding chunks of rock.

Another strategy meeting was held. After a final reaming of the hole, the group decided not to risk using any of the three capsules for the rescue attempt. Engineers feared the pods, nearly as wide as the escape hole, could become stuck, trapping the men a second time. Lodged in the tight circumference, the trapped miners would certainly meet a claustrophobic end inside these death tombs.

The capsule - project was immediately abandoned and another plan formulated. At that point, the decision was made to bring the miners to the surface in body harness coveralls attached to a thick lift cable. The coveralls would help protect the miners from the sides of the jagged borehole. Skydivers David Price and Don Kellner were consulted to help design a set of coveralls with parachute harnesses sewn inside.

The harness was modified to suit the exact physical sizes of the trapped miners. It was then sewn to coveralls modeled by men approximately the same size as Fellin and Throne. This was done to expedite the rescue process. Each man would don his respective coveralls and thus automatically have most of the harness in place, saving valuable time. Three sets of the coveralls were made.

After several hours of preparation, the two sets of parachute harnesses and sturdy coveralls were simultaneously lowered into the mine chamber. Fellin and Throne were instructed to help each other into the complicated rescue gear, making certain that the straps were straight and not tangled or disconnected.

A large bucket of axle grease was lowered into the chamber. The men were coached to apply the thick lubricant to their outer clothing. This would allow them to slide easier through the narrow structure. The miners took turns smearing gobs of the grease over each other's arms, shoulders and hips. The grease would make the tight trip to freedom a little easier as the diameter of the borehole was only a claustrophobic 17-½ inches wide.

Body modification

Mining is a treacherous profession. It takes its toll upon even the strongest of men. After years of shoveling coal, the physical aches and pains, and strained muscles, became familiar companions. David Fellin had flecks of coal embedded under his skin. The coal transformed his face into a display of tribal body modification. One could read the years of struggle in his wrinkled, hardened countenance.

It made sense for Fellin to be the last one out of the damned pit. He insisted that Throne be rescued first. Fellin decided that this would be easier for the highly emotional Throne, rather than have him languish at the bottom of the slope, alone with his demons.

Throne's hallucinations

Hank Throne was a young and emotionally charged lad. He was primed to explode when least expected. He had already lost control numerous times. Throne later recounted the time when he became overcome with anger during their entombment. He started to scream at Fellin, "I must have been off my rocker a little," he reluctantly admitted. "I yelled at Davey --- 'Dave, I'm going home, I'm going alone, if you don't want to come." In a state of panic, Throne screamed in anguish when the rescuers had not made contact. He thought they had given up.

On another occasion, Throne experienced what might have been vivid hallucinations: "I saw a door. 'Davey,' I yelled, 'let's go there.' I crawled toward it but suddenly found myself bumping into another piece of timber. I got a bruise under my eye. I was so frightened, I just went wild. I crawled like mad away from Dave and fell into a hole. I found myself yelling as loud as I could and the echo came bouncing back to me. Exhaustion is what finally calmed me."

Fellin talked him through that one, too. He lowered his voice and spoke calmly and slowly. His voice had a relaxing effect on Throne. Fellin would be called upon to do it again, just before Throne's extrication.

Fellin encouraged his partner, telling him that he could do this. He was almost home. "Annie's waiting for you," Fellin said. "She has a cold beer waiting for you."

A plan had been made. The rescuers provided detailed instructions on how to secure the harnesses, which took almost an hour. The moment had finally arrived. Now the miners had to exert patience and trust. Their lives were in the hands of those topside.

Each had a microphone around his neck, so that two-way communications could be maintained with each miner while they were being hoisted through the borehole. Each wore a thick padded collar, tightly draped around their neck and a protective helmet. Fellin looked over Throne's parachute assembly for the last time. Everything seemed to be in order. It was about 1:45 a.m. and time to go.

Hank Throne was instructed to place his arms above his head, next to his helmet, in the event that he passed out during the extrication. Throne lifted his arms over his head and stuffed them inside the borehole. He could feel the narrow circumference of the borehole pressed against his body. His arms were stretched above his head, tightly against the orange helmet.

The rescue team instructed him through a microphone. They wanted him to remain calm. Just relax and enjoy the ride, they said. Throne felt himself slowly being lifted, crushed against the sides of the borehole. "I'm coming up. I'm coming up," he shouted, fear and excitement creeping into his voice. The operators stopped the winch, not wanting to injure him or twist the special safety harness straps.

Claustrophobia

For some, claustrophobia is a condition considered worse than death. Being hauled vertically through the borehole was, in many ways, a more severe horror than being entombed in the cavern. Throne was petrified.

The thick cable tightened and began to tug him upwards, slowly, through the narrow opening. His arms stretched to the point of near impossibility, and he feared that his limbs would be torn from their screaming sockets. He felt throbbing, continuous pain. His anterior shoulder and upper arm muscles burned in response to the maneuver. He struggled to slow down his heartbeat, to relax, but was unable to control the creature that snarled inside his chest and threatened to rupture his heart.

As he gasped for breath, a dry heave lodged in his parched throat. He began to hyperventilate. His body whipped and twisted pretzel-like in slow motion as he was pulled upward. Throne's heart began to pound, his mind racing, as the harness encircled him and slowly spun him around. A violent tug forced him sideways into the wall. The parched skin around his lips blanched in fear. His body shook uncontrollably. Throne tried to maintain control, as a choking sense of terror, a dizzying nausea, filled him.

The heavy cable lurched back and forth against the winch. Throne was yanked upwards. He found himself wedged against the wall, stunned, but unhurt. His body began to turn in a dizzying circle, the straps twisted in an impossible maze. "I'm turning around a bit now. Still turning around," he screamed. "Go ahead. I'm still turning around." Throne was sweating, his heart screaming. Adrenaline seared acid-like in his veins.

His nostrils burned.

Clouds of dust and minute coal particles singed as they were sucked in and out of his lungs. A musty smell filled his nose. The air smelled strangely of ozone and negative ions. Throne sucked moisture and dust motes into his gasping lungs.

He was being pulled by the bulky straps and heaved against the irregular sides of the borehole. Throne drifted upwards, further and further into an unknown void. It was the twilight membrane between irrational sensation and insanity. He had never experienced anything like this; the numbing vibration and slow motion spinning. The human mind needs to find meaning, needs to fill in the blank spaces. Throne had lots of time to think. Would he live or die? He believed that he was in purgatory waiting to be summoned to Hell.

It took him 15 minutes and 45 seconds to be pulled from the bottom of the pit to the top of the slope. In his mind that torment lasted several lifetimes. He reached the top at 2:03 a.m. as the smell of fresh, cool air rushed over him and he was lugged out of the borehole. There were hands all over him, spiderlike, pulling and tugging at his helmet and grease-covered coveralls. Finally he sensed the hard earth under his feet. He shook. Throne clutched the sides of his head with shaking hands as an anguished cry escaped from his lips and he collapsed into a stretcher.

He would later recall that moment: "Finally, there it was – the surface, the air, the people," said an elated Hank Throne. "As the air hit me, I felt dizzy and fell into that basket-type stretcher. I was thinking I'm out now, I'm out now, and I cried for the first time," he said. The cool air, he recalled, hit him hard and knocked him out.

A bearded, hardened Dave Fellin was the next to be rescued. He wore a blue helmet and coveralls, stained by gobs of thick grease. Fellin began his ascent at 2:33 a.m. It took him eight minutes and 15 seconds, almost half the time taken by Throne. As they pulled him through the borehole he did not disappoint the crowd and began to sing "She'll be comin' round the mountain." Fellin was laughing and making jokes, "This is the best ride I ever had," he quipped. The rescuers later revealed that Fellin's courage was fueled by a few gulps of Johnnie Walker, covertly sent down the borehole prior to his rescue.

Fellin was out of the hole at 2:41 a.m.

Anna greeted him, hugged him and began to cry. Fellin pleaded, "Don't cry, Anna. I'm all right, I'm all right."

The next moments unfolded precipitously, dreamlike. The miners were escorted to a pair of U.S. Marine Corps helicopters, parked on a hastily prepared landing strip. The transport helicopter had been converted to combat search and rescue and medical evacuation. It hovered, blades ferociously spinning, a whirling thunder of hope and apprehension. It lofted, birdlike, making a wide circle and soaring at 105 miles per hour to the Hazleton State General Hospital. The first one transported Throne. Dr. Anthony Fedullo, Fellin's physician, accompanied his patient in the second airship.

Several days after their rescue on August 27, the miners were released from the hospital. It had been almost two weeks before the Sheppton disaster, observed through an international lens, reached this miraculous conclusion.

During their hospitalization, both miners believed that Bova was still alive. No one seemed to be listening.

Attempts to locate Bova had been cancelled after officials estimated it would take another 120 days to reach the spot where the miner was believed to be located. Secretary Charmbury said it was "too hazardous to risk the life of anyone" in attempting to find Bova. Ultimately, a court order to retrieve Bova's body was rescinded. Now it was time for the grieving Eva Bova to end her vigil. The overwrought miner's wife, admitted to the Shenandoah State General Hospital, was exhausted and without hope.

Still, others celebrated the moment. President John F. Kennedy sent a telegram to the survivors. It stated, "Congratulations! The stamina, courage and spirit which you and your rescuers have exhibited in recent days have earned the admiration of all Americans. I wish to join with them in expressing my heartfelt good wishes for your speedy recovery."

The glow of celebration soon dimmed, snuffed out like a church candle as grotesque allegations of human depravity rose, specter like. And as they walked upon solid ground for the first time, the miners embraced little realization that the worst was yet to come.

Chapter 8
PARALLEL UNIVERSE

What the entombed miners experienced was something the human mind endures only through hallucinations and insanity. The Sheppton ordeal was different. Sheppton was not an idealized dream state but the worst possible nightmare; a parallel universe of terror cloaked in stark reality.

It was a reality that mental health professionals would investigate, questioning and analyzing Fellin and Throne, searching for answers as to the limits of human endurance.

Now observed like rats in a wire maze, their entombment became a macabre scientific experiment. The questions were all similar. *Can you describe what it was like after the initial cave-in? How did you react? Take your time. Try to remember everything.*

Fellin stepped forward and articulated their story in a mesmerizing and consistent manner. He became both emissary and scribe. Fellin described the grinding sound of a locomotive roaring towards them. Chunks of rock and coal rained down like an ocean riptide, the rumble amplified by the sound of screaming. He crumpled to the bottom of the ground, the floor vibrating angrily. It felt as though it was alive and moving under his feet. Everything was happening fast. There were more rushes. They tried to count how long it lasted but the reverberations continued for days upon days. They were being punished, existing in a state of trauma, a place devoid of calm.

The world was spellbound to learn how the men had survived? Fellin and Throne's triumph was of utmost concern to U.S. Navy physician Lt. Richard Anderson, of the Naval Medical Research Institute in Bethesda, Maryland. Anderson was a specialist in survival techniques. He had been conducting studies with individuals isolated in bomb shelters for lengthy periods of time and explained that they had lived under those conditions "without serious problems."

But on the other hand, he pointed out, the bomb shelter survivors had lived in excellent conditions with adequate stores of food, water and controlled room temperatures. For Fellin and Throne, this was not the case; still, Anderson observed that, "The men seem to be in fairly good physical condition, but it's difficult to give a more exact assessment of their condition..." As far as their psychological state of mind, Anderson said: "It's a tribute to their guts that they haven't given up yet. The fact that they're in as good a shape as they are – that they never gave up – is pretty good news. They're pretty tough boys.

"As long as there's food, water and hope--they're going to get along fairly well," Anderson concluded.

According to experts like Anderson, survival depended on prior preparation and the ability of an individual or individuals to remain calm and work together toward a common goal. Fellin the mentor, and Throne, his student, immediately established a bond, a pact to find a way out of this pit of hell. To that end, both articulated what their survival strategy should be.

It was direct and uncomplicated and initiated by Fellin: "Hank, let's sit down and talk this over and see what we can do," he said as they suffered in the darkness. "Let's do something. Let's get out of here," was Throne's reply.

Throne watched. He listened in amazement as Fellin spoke of God and Jesus. There was something heroic and seemingly superhuman about David Fellin, 30-years his senior. He possessed an internal peace and stillness, refusing to allow the unfolding chaos to disturb him. He was unwilling to expend negative energy on Sheppton's punishing hellhole. Instead, Fellin became more serene and less angry, more focused and less confused.

Henry Throne believed that Fellin saved his life. He claimed that if it wasn't for the comfort and reassurance of Fellin, he wouldn't have made it through the horrific psychological ordeal. The men prayed together. They also systematically began to dig upwards, digging out an area estimated at about 20 feet in length with a few tools that they luckily found.

World dissolving

Faith, conservation of energy and focus on a goal became their salvation. It became their Holy Trinity. They dug, prayed and tapped. Miners always tapped. The sound would carry and reverberate deep through the mineshafts, letting the world know they were still alive. Having lost electrical power and phone contact, it was the miner's sole means of communication.

After their rescue, the miners were interviewed at the Hazleton State Hospital. Authorities wanted to know exactly how the duo was able to survive those six days before the miraculous breakthrough. Fellin explained with clarity how they were able to endure. His recollections were coherent and detailed. He said,

"We found a hatchet with a broken handle, a crowbar, and a saw that wouldn't saw. We found an old rasp and I used it to file the saw and sharpen the hatchet. Now we were back in business. We had some tools to probe around. Now we could look for a way out. But we never found one," he emphasized.

After the cave-in, Fellin immediately took inventory and calculated their fate. Lunch pails and water jugs had been lost under tons of debris. A blanket of hopelessness covered him in waves of despondency. Their carbide lamps would last only a few more hours. Suddenly devoid of color, Fellin saw their world dissolving into shadows of grays and blacks, before he stared into a mass of incomprehensible darkness. The darkness scared him but, somehow, they both got used to the gloom and found a way to navigate their way slowly around the cavern.

They persisted. And improvised. "I found a four-foot-long pipe lying there, said Fellin. "I plugged up one end with electrical tape that I had in my pocket. Then I shoved a piece of cable through it, tying it at the other end. Then I jammed some rags into that end. Then I dropped the pipe into the drainage hole and when I pulled it up we had a four-foot pipe filled with water. Sure, it was sulfur water, but it was water that would keep us alive.

"The first time we tried it we spit it out. The second time it stayed down. I told Hank to drink only a quarter swallow at a time. We had to ration it," he explained.

Fire and water

The first rule of law: Blood draws. Everyone knew that. The old reporters joked, "If it bleeds, it leads." Sheppton was a prime example. They came like vultures, hovering in droves, circling overhead, ravenously hungry and sensing the kill. The sharks, the cameras and the media.

After the ordeal, Fellin would tell and then retell his story. How many times would they force him to relive the horror? They posed the same questions, again and again, asked by different people with unusual facial expressions and dissimilar degrees of intensity. They squinted at him queer-eyed, patronizing, condescending, and insincere. They looked at him as one might inspect a bug under a magnifying glass. It was similar, he thought, to a torture scene from a black and white monster movie.

Dave Fellin knew the story well, could recite it backwards and forwards. It got better in the retelling. The newspapers and television and radio people wanted a story of triumph over impossible odds. They wanted the nasty stuff, the part that the world had never heard before. That's what he gave them. He told them how his body seized up, muscles strained, clenched, his jaw locked in a spasm of fear. He had never felt such terror before. The darkness wrapped around him in a strangulation hold that threatened to destroy his sanity. He felt he was going mad. So this is what it was like. Head spinning, swirling, unable to comprehend.

He gave them more.

The newspaper journalists asked personal questions, pushing past delicate boundaries of dignity and decency. They forced Fellin to relive the horror. He heard himself answering, as an alien voice responded. Yes, they went to the bathroom down there. The sour reek of stale urine was always present, mixed with millions of spinning dust particles, part coal dust and unbreathable air.

Reporters swarmed. Flashbulbs popped. The correspondents persisted.

You seem to have survived the ordeal quite well. Was there anything that really scared you down in the mine?

Fellin was ready for the question. Yes, he admitted, "There were only two things that frightened me down there. They were fire and water.

Fellin admitted that he was afraid of being electrocuted, and afraid of being drowned. The cave-in had severed the electric lines that dangled down into the slope. Any contact with water would lead to instant death. Pockets of water, released by the rescue drills, could rush through the borehole and flood the monkey shaft.

Down there, death had many faces.

The public hungered for every little scrap of information – myth, folklore, or legend - that told of mine disasters. Accounts of mine survivors became valuable currency. Around the time of the Sheppton tragedy, a little-known incident, that transpired 72 - years earlier, was reported by the Pottsville *Republican*. It was a saga of fellow miners who, presumed to be dead, had beat impossible odds.

The Jeansville Disaster occurred February 4, 1891, and has been called one of the most "remarkable events in the history of mining." The No. 1 slope was located near the south boundary of Luzerne County and about two-miles south of Hazleton. At 10:50 a.m. two miners, Patrick Colt and Charles Boyle, were at work in a breast of the mine. They were drilling a hole and struck a vast body of water. In a few moments the entire slope was flooded. In less than five minutes the rushing water raised 624 feet to the mouth of the slope. Eighteen men were suddenly swallowed by surging water and helplessly drowned.

At the time of the accident there were 25 men working in the slope. One of the seven who escaped said that initially there was a rumble like the sound of an approaching train. In a moment there was a fierce blast of wind and the lamps were extinguished. There was a frantic cry, "For God's sake run for your lives!"

A Pennsylvania Department of Mines report for 1891 tells of the survival of four men trapped under 140 feet of water when water from one mine broke into the workings of another. Ten men were drowned. Four men survived entombment for 19 days and eight hours at the Spring Mountain Colliery, Jeanesville. When the water was pumped out, Joseph Matusowski, John Pomasuzewis, Wasil Frinko and John Barno were found alive. One report stated that "all perished except four, who in this darkness of horror survived twenty days and were finally rescued and recovered from the dreadful experience."

A History of the Coal Miners of the United States described the ordeal in this manner: "The four men had been 18 days underground. For some days they had eaten sparingly of the dinner they had taken in the mine on the morning of their imprisonment. When this food was exhausted, they drank oil and ate rats, which like themselves had sought safety from the flood in the higher workings. The prisoners suffered from cold, and rubbed themselves against each other to restore warmth. The stronger of the four was known as 'Big Joe' Matusowski and it was he who kept knocking on the pillar in the hope of attracting the attention of the rescuers. All four, by careful nursing and medical attendance, recovered."

The Kingdom of Coal also revealed the miners' extraordinary survival, although they listed their number as "five." "After 20-days five men were found alive in a breast; they had managed to survive by eating parts of their clothing and chewing bark from the timber. Eventually six bodies also were discovered, eaten by rats almost beyond recognition."

The survivors, after treatment in hospitals, all recovered. The outspoken critics soon charged that the accident could have been prevented. They blamed the mining engineers for not notifying the miners of the proximity of the large body of water. The mine was operated by T.C. Hayden and Company, which also operated mines in Mahanoy City, PA. The superintendent of the colliery at that time was a Pottsville man, John Womelsdorf.

Unforgiving environment

It was Tuesday, September 3, 1963, when Fellin and Throne were discharged from Hazleton State Hospital, amid a horde of media and intrusive reporters. Flashbulbs exploded everywhere. Seemingly a million years earlier, they had survived against all odds from their cursed entombment. That, too, was on a Tuesday: August 13, 1963.

During that two-week period, Fellin did everything he could to ensure the survival of his co-worker. Throne needed the help and support of the older miner. Although the drill broke through on the sixth day, and provided some comfort, the slope remained oppressive, an unforgiving environment.

Around the 10th day, Fellin reported to the rescue team about the continued harsh conditions. He said, "We're doing everything we can think of to keep warm. We're very cold and Hank's hands are beginning to swell."

How did they survive? Fellin didn't know. Maybe it was the power of prayer. He prayed constantly and encouraged Throne to do the same. Fellin tried to stay positive and purge dark thoughts from his mind. He tried not to focus on the fact that the rescuers were taking far too long. They should have been reached by now. It was almost a week without contact. Throne was able to calculate how long it would take them to drill down to the monkey shaft. He hoped that at some point they would be rescued. He believed that they would be rescued.

Maybe some primitive part of his brain had been stimulated, transmuting him into a creature intent upon survival and nothing else.

He had no further explanation.

Chapter 9
THE UNSPEAKABLE

As Throne, and then Fellin, were pulled out of the godforsaken pit, throngs of onlookers began to yell and scream. It was the moment they had all prayed for. Over 100 miners, rescue team members and support personnel witnessed the unfolding miracle. It was an incredible celebration captured through an international lens and instantaneously broadcast around the world. The Coal Region's finest hour would be frozen in time, replayed over and over again. It was a solitary example of man overcoming impossible odds.

Then the cruel reality set in.

The applause died and, as the cheers slowly diminished, there was the urgent matter of Louis Bova to be considered. Something had to be done.

After another 12-inch hole was drilled, the rescue team dropped microphones and a television camera deep into the borehole. No sounds were detected but a camera revealed a blurred image of what appeared to be a person sitting against a wooden mine prop in an upright position. The individual was stationary. No movement was detected.

Secretary of Mines H. Beecher Charmberry observed, "It appears to be --- and you have to be very careful about this – appears to be a man's body down there. We are by no means sure of this."

Fellin and Bova's brother Dan were skeptical that his body would be in the same chamber that had entombed the two miners. There was only one way to find out if Louis Bova was down there.

In stepped Andrew Drebitko.

Drebitko, an officer of the Independent Miners Association, immediately volunteered and demanded that he be lowered into the mining chamber. Drebitko's emotional appeal would conjure up yet another of Sheppton's mysteries. As a means of protecting his family, the officials decided to keep Drebitko's identity secret. The rescue team referred to Drebitko as "Mr. Rescue Volunteer." Later, Sheppton author James A. Goodman, christened him as the mysterious "Mr. X."

At the borehole site, thick tarps were hoisted upon wooden slabs and nailed tight to prevent anyone from seeing Drebitko prior to his descent into the hole. It became a further aspect of the Sheppton mythology. Drebitko, hidden inside a truck, was driven to the hole. With a blanket draped over his head he was lifted out of the vehicle and led to the hole by two rescue team members. There he was placed inside the tarp-covered entrance to the borehole.

Drebitko was carefully and slowly lowered into the dank cavity with the snug parachute harness. He was filled both with optimism and dread. Upon reaching the bottom he found a plug used to close up the 12-inch bore hole, a piece of rope that looked like human hair and a miner's helmet placed on the top. That was the image the camera had picked up. He found no bones, clothing or proof that Bova had been there.

Hope was fading. The mood of celebration and expectation became atrabilious. Although some believed Bova could still be alive, trapped more than 300 feet underground, Charmbury said that it "was too hazardous to risk the life of anyone" to continue the rescue operation. Additionally, Charmbury estimated that it would take 120 days to reach the position where Fellin believed Bova was trapped. 120 days was a death sentence. A court order to retrieve Bova's body was rescinded.

The Sheppton Mythology

Immediately, allegations of government incompetence and corruption blended with barroom rumors of cannibalism. The Sheppton Mythology swirled. Everyone seemed to have a theory. People began to talk, trying to explain what had happened to Bova. He couldn't have just disappeared.

"Evil men," Fellin snapped at an interviewer who repeated the accusations of cannibalism. It was another baited attempt to provoke Fellin to react emotionally and provide them a juicy quote. "That's what they are. Only evil men could think that I could have eaten Bova to stay alive."

Fellin was referring to an outrageous article published in a 1968 Chicago *Daily News* feature. The article regurgitated barroom gossip insinuating that miners, in times of life or death, would sacrifice the smallest of their team. At five feet, four inches tall, Louis Bova was the smallest of the three and weighed a modest 120 pounds. Those statistics appeared to be proof enough for those promoting the horrible rumor as truth.

Throne was even more direct, although, in hindsight, he should have simply avoided the question and said nothing. "I don't even like meat," he awkwardly explained to the rapacious media.

Regarding the incident at Sheppton, some questioned how the two miners could have survived without food rations. The reality of their plight was obvious; an exploratory drill reached them after five days. Prior to that, they survived by swilling sulfur water and eating wood splinters. Much of those days were filled with traumatic stress and a dramatic lack of appetite. Their only goal was to survive for another 24 hours.

But, like a spider's web, speculation begat rumor, accusation and folklore. Because of that suspicion, like other coal region legends, a repugnant mythology slowly assumed shape.

Just a Coincidence

The rationale for cannibalism is gruesome and mind-boggling and seemingly unimaginable. It harbors much variation as it includes elements of survival, control, psychosis and spirituality.

A further element seethed within the pages of Tennessee William's *Suddenly, Last Summer*. In the popular motion picture adaptation, Sebastian Venable is torn apart and eaten. Venable, a homosexual predator, is chased through the streets of *Cabeza de Lobo* and then eaten alive by a ravenous mob of young boys. According to Williams, that horrific scene was meant, metaphorically and not literally. It later became an item of contention between Williams' intent and Hollywood's interpretation and, much later, played a part in the song "Timothy's" composition. The popularity of "Timothy," released in 1971 and sung and played by The Buoys, a Northeastern Pennsylvania rock band, was due in part to its perceived connection with rumors of cannibalism surrounding the Sheppton mine cave-in eight years before.

However, the Keystone Record Collector's B. Derek Shaw disputed this possible connection when he broke down the elements of "Timothy's" genesis: "The inspiration for Holmes' tune was from two other sources: the popular Tennessee Ernie Ford tune, "Sixteen Tons" (Capitol, 1955) and the 1959 Tennessee Williams play, *Suddenly, Last Summer*, which touches on cannibalism. He merged the two themes together, writing the song from a first person perspective. (Jimmy Dean's) "Big Bad John" (Columbia, 1961) is also a similar story.

"I doubt Holmes knew anything about the Sheppton disaster that occurred eight years prior. It was just a coincidence. Holmes, from the New York City metro area, was looking to write a song that would potentially get banned, generating more interest in The Buoys, the group that ended up recording it. That idea worked.

Shaw elaborated on his perspective regarding the intent of the composition: "The song is a realistic attempt, in a first person narrative, to explain what could happen, but never coming out stating 'cannibalism.' The song borders on a psychological study when people are left in a confined area.

"Again Rupert Holmes never patterned the song after the Sheppton Mining Disaster," Shaw emphasized.

Implied Possibility

The implied possibility of cannibalism wasn't novel, particularly if one were familiar with the Donner Party incident. In 1846, the Donner-Reed Party attempted to reach California via wagon train using a presumed shorter route, but became trapped in the Sierra Nevada Mountains.

To survive, the 81 pioneers ate bones, twigs, string, hides and a concoction described as "glue." They also ate their family dog "Cash." Emigrant Virginia Reed Murphy wrote, "We ate his head and feet --- hide --- everything about him." Mrs. Georgia Donner, one of the remaining

47, claimed that human flesh was cooked for all members of the Donner Party, but was given only to the children. Her dubious claim has never been fully substantiated.

Another tale, perhaps steeped more in folklore than stark reality, was that of legendary cannibal Alferd Packer. He was accused of the unspeakable during the winter of 1873-1874. Convicted of manslaughter, Packer was sentenced to 40-years in prison for allegedly eating five of his fellow prospectors, lost in the Rocky Mountains. Drenched in notoriety, Packer joins real-life cannibals Armin Meiwes, Alexander Pearce, Jeffrey Dahmer and Albert Fish, in the forensic lineup of this aberrant group of pathogens.

Flight 571

Examples of the unspeakable are more common than many realize. The 1993 motion picture *Alive* portrayed the October 13, 1972, crash of Uruguayan Air Force Flight 571. Among those aboard were 45 individuals, including the Uruguayan Old Christians Rugby Team, all dreadfully imprisoned in sub-zero temperatures in the remote, snowbound Andes. Trapped at an altitude of 11,800 feet, the 16 survivors fed on dead passengers who had been miraculously preserved in the frozen snow.

In his 2006 book, *Miracles in the Andes: 72 Days on the Mountain and My Long Trek Home*, Nando Parrado reflected on his ordeal: "At high altitude, the body's caloric needs are astronomical ... we were starving in earnest, with no hope of finding food, but our hunger soon grew so voracious that we searched anyway ...again and again we scoured the fuselage in search of crumbs and morsels. We tried to eat strips of leather torn from pieces of luggage, though we knew that the chemicals they'd been treated with would do us more harm than good. We ripped open seat cushions hoping to find straw, but found only inedible upholstery foam ... Again and again I came to the same conclusion: unless we wanted to eat the clothes we were wearing, there was nothing here but aluminum, plastic, ice, and rock."

Researchers including Piers Paul Read, who wrote *Alive: The Story of the Andes Survivors* (1974), concluded that because all of the passengers were Roman Catholic, they rationalized their act of necrotic cannibalism as being morally correct and equivalent to the ritual of Holy Communion or Eucharist. "Transubstantiation," the official Roman Catholic concept referring to the change that takes place during the sacrament of Holy Communion, involves the substances of bread and wine being turned miraculously into the body and blood of Christ himself.

The Biblical verse in John 6:55, "For my flesh is meat indeed, and my blood is drink indeed," appeared to be the words that addressed their dilemma, while another, John 15:13, reads "No man hath greater love than this: that he lay down his life for his friends."

A more-recent incident, with uncanny similarities, occurred on August 5, 2010, after 33 Chilean coalminers were trapped 2,295 feet underground inside the San Jose Mine in northern Chili's Atacama Desert.

The miners remained trapped in sweltering heat for 69 days. During that initial phase, they had to conserve what little food stores they had. Every 48-hours, each man received a ration of two teaspoonfuls of tuna, half a glass of milk and half a cookie. They knew that at some point the food supplies would be exhausted. In the early days of their ordeal, the possibility of cannibalism was discussed as a means of survival.

Mario Sepulveda, interviewed by author Jonathan Franklin, reflected, "It was no joke, there was no more food. But how long before cannibalism became a very realistic option? I would say five or 10 days. Food or no food, I was going to get out of there ... I had to think about which miner was going to collapse first and then started thinking about how I was going to eat him ... I wasn't embarrassed, I wasn't scared."

Another miner who survived the ordeal, Samuel Avalos, explained to Chile's *TVN* public television network, "It was kind of who died first, that's where we were, he who died first ... the rest will go there, like the little animals."

900-Day Siege

Cannibalism was evident as one of the more sordid chapters of World War II unfolded on September 8, 1941. The

Siege of Leningrad, also known as the 900-Day Siege, began after German and Finnish forces advanced against the USSR's second largest city. Enemy forces surrounded Leningrad. All supply lines, including precious food rations, were cut off. After all pets, birds and rats had been eaten, predatory gangs resorted to extreme measures. Unfortunate pedestrians were stalked, attacked and their human flesh consumed. These horrific acts of cannibalism were reported in the winter of 1941–1942.

As described by *History.com:* "Residents burned books and furniture to stay warm and searched for food to supplement their scarce rations. Animals from the city zoo were consumed early in the siege, followed before long by household pets. Wallpaper paste made from potatoes was scraped off the wall, and leather was boiled to produce an edible jelly. Grass and weeds were cooked, and scientists worked to extract vitamins from pine needles and tobacco dust. Hundreds, perhaps thousands, resorted to cannibalizing the dead, and in a few cases people were murdered for their flesh. The Leningrad police struggled to keep order and formed a special division to combat cannibalism."

That squad uncovered human carcasses draped on meat hooks in gruesome smelling frozen food lockers. More than one million Leningrad citizens perished during the Nazi siege, lasting from 1941 to 1944. In the aftermath, over 260 Leningraders were imprisoned for the crime of cannibalism.

Odd Chapter

In *The Famous Sheppton Mine Rescue*, J. Ronnie Sando penned an odd chapter called "A Cry of Cannibalism." It read in part, " ... when word got out, all of a sudden a rescue as great as this was marred by the outcry from the press and people of *cannibalism*. It's really something how the opinions of people change.

"Being a young man at the time I couldn't believe what I was hearing and I had a sick feeling inside. The same crowds that were cheering the rescue on were now screaming that they (Fellin and Throne) ate Louie Bova while they were entombed; they were calling them cannibals. I remember later seeing a headline from one of the papers and in big bold black letters it read 'CANNIBALISM.'"

"Immediately Dave Fellin and Hank Throne were put under State Police guard at the state hospital. I still had a sick feeling in my stomach because of the people's outcries, but I knew these two miners on a personal basis and I knew this couldn't be true; anyway I sure hoped it wasn't.

"I felt strongly that the charges and outcries of what they were being accused of had to be false. Dave Fellin was a hard-working, honest person and a good God-fearing man and wouldn't do something of that nature to another human being or let it happen on his watch."

"There were people saying that Fellin and Throne resorted to cannibalism to survive," Sando said. "The State Police did investigate and Andrew Drabitko, who was the head of the Independent Miners Association, was lowered into the shaft to look for Bova's body."

The special camera, that was lowered into the area where Thorne and Fellin had been entombed, captured what appeared to be a human body wearing a miner's hat. Drabitko's mission was to go underground and investigate the contents of the mineshaft.

What Drabitko discovered was not made of flesh and blood. The image was actually a pile of dirty clothing and an old wooden mine prop. Either Fellin or Throne had placed a helmet on top of the structure as the rescue crew was hoisting them to freedom. The makeshift manikin looked like the body of a human being. The rescue crew's initial speculation was that it was the corpse of Louis Bova, but, as of this date, the remains of Bova have never been found and will remain buried beneath the streets of Sheppton.

Surprisingly, J. Ronnie Sando surmises that because no remains were found, cannibalism was not a factor in Bova's death. He reasoned, "There was no body. This immediately cleared Dave and Hank of all the accusations of cannibalism leveled against them." Sando's argument of "No body, no crime" is flawed. This archaic English decree implied that a suspect could not be charged with murder without the victim's body as evidence. The law has since been refuted, and, as one example, the United States case of *People v. Scott* [1960] held that "circumstantial evidence, when sufficient to exclude every other reasonable hypothesis, may prove the death of a missing person, the existence of a homicide and the guilt of the accused". Although accusations of cannibalism were never argued in a Schuylkill County courtroom, the court of public opinion had already rendered its verdict.

Everyone offered an opinion about the missing body. News reporter and talk show host L.A. Tarone was quick to address part of that mystique. "Sheppton was quite the story. That they never found Bova's body has struck many as sort of eerie. I don't think it was at all. Sheppton was the latest, and last, in a long series of mine cave-ins around here. In almost all those cases, they never recovered all the bodies. When there's a cave-in, geology changes – veins shift, holes open, things fall. It wasn't that unusual at all – tragic yes, unusual, not really."

There were no charges of cannibalism filed and that morbid speculation was "officially" put to rest. Although Bova's body was never recovered, the fierce debate smoldered and raged as accusation and conjecture thrived in smoky barrooms, in the lyrics of a controversial song and in the tortured mind of a miners' son.

John Bova was only eight months old when his father disappeared. Young John Bova learned about his father through vile accusation and inference. He grew up with rumors and allegations about cannibalism. The young Bova told Hazleton *Standard Speaker* staff writer Kelly Monitz, "All my life, they said (Fellin and Throne) ate my father. "To this day, I wonder if they ate him," John Bova questioned. "Now the only one that knows is God, because everyone else is dead."

Louis Bova's son, John, believes that his father died a gruesome death. He believes that his father was eaten. He told this writer that Uncle Joe, his Dad's brother, revealed this grotesque allegation to him. Uncle Joe told young Bova that his dad had most likely been cannibalized, his remains hidden.

"No one will ever know the truth. It was taken with them," Bova said. "What was the truth?" We can only assume." "I live with it every day. My mother was never the same." Eva Bova had dealt with depression, poor health and kidney operations her entire life. She rarely spoke of the disaster. Her infrequent speech muted by uncontrolled crying. She denied the ugly accusations. Eva Bova cried every day. Eva passed away in 2002.

Chapter 10
TIMOTHY

Trapped in a mine that had caved in and everyone knows the only ones left, was Joe and me and Tim.

When they broke through to pull us free, the only ones left to tell the tale, was Joe ... and me.

Timothy, Timothy, where on earth did you go, Timothy, Timothy, God why don't I know.

Hungry as hell... no food to eat and Joe said that he would sell his soul for just...a piece...of meat

Water enough to drink for two and Joe said to me, I'll take a swig, and then...there's some...for you.

Timothy, Timothy, Joe was looking at you, Timothy, Timothy, God what did we do.

I must have blacked out just about then cause the very next thing that I could see was the light of the day again.

My stomach was full as it could be and nobody ever got around to finding...Timothy.

Timothy, Timothy, where on earth did you go,
Timothy, Timothy, God why don't I know.
Timothy………yea….

"Timothy," written by Rupert Holmes. Copyright 1971 by Jordan-Herman-Holmes Publishing Inc., and Universal Music Corporation (ASCAP). All rights reserved.

The plaintive song combined elements of a mining disaster with the enigmatic hint of cannibalism. Because many assumed that "Timothy" was about Sheppton, that fictitious and baseless interpretation (in this writer's opinion) spread throughout the patches like a black pestilence, like a biblical plague.

"Timothy" began as a clever marketing scheme between Rupert Holmes and C. Michael Wright and resulted in one of the most controversial songs ever recorded. At the time, Holmes was a struggling 20-year-old songwriter working for Scepter Records. He had been in the record business for almost a year, willing to do just about anything to succeed in the competitive industry.

Luckily, Wright, a junior engineer at Scepter Records, had an invaluable inside connection. On weekends he had access to an extra set of keys that unlocked the vacant confines of the Scepter recording studio. That fortuitous break allowed Wright and Holmes to experiment with the evolving music technology and record songs. Together, the pair forged an innovative creative unit, their potential keenly observed by Scepter, which sensed the possibility. A deal was made, the proverbial no brainer. Scepter agreed to take a chance and release one single produced by Holmes and Wright.

Wright's immediate mission was to locate a rock act to record their song. Being familiar with musical talent in Northeastern Pennsylvania, he soon discovered The Buoys, an exciting group from Wilkes-Barre. The Buoys had developed a well deserved reputation for musicality and solid stage performance. Although they dabbled in early garage rock, The Buoys evolved far beyond that limited format. They were recognized for their note-for-note perfect renditions of Beatles' songs and, later, the intricate harmonies of Crosby, Stills, Nash & Young, all before creating their rendition of the Great American Rock Song. Their electrifying act, featuring the soaring vocals of Bill Kelly, included screaming fans, sold out auditoriums and standing-room-only crowds. It was a snapshot of the Buoys at their finest hour, launching into an adventure that, despite the odds, would only get better.

The Recording Session

Although Wright understood that Scepter would not promote their song, he wanted to make the most of the opportunity. Rupert Holmes had an idea. He suggested that The Buoys record a song that would get banned. That way,

SHEPPTON: THE MYTH, MIRACLE & MUSIC

there would be some debate about the group and, hopefully, another label would sign and promote them. With that strategy in mind, Holmes crafted a provocative song he expected to get blacklisted from commercial radio, but garner both controversy and airplay from other less conservative stations.

At New York City-based Scepter studios, Holmes introduced "Timothy" to the Buoys by playing it on a grand piano. Although he envisioned the final take as an up-tempo Creedence Clearwater Revival sound, he presented it initially as a slowed-down funeral dirge. All of the group members contributed to the dynamic creative process, with instruments, vocals and harmonies.

After the song was recorded, C. Michael Wright "sweetened" the tune by adding horns, strings and precision orchestration. Some liked the finished product; , others didn't. Nonetheless, the enhanced effects gave the straight-forward rock song additional range, setting it apart from many previous musical productions of the era.

Bob Gryziac was the original bass player on the "Timothy" recording, but just before the song's release, Gryziac abruptly quit the band. Several other members also left. The Scepter LP was finally completed with a new, revised lineup consisting of Fran Brozena, Chris Hanlon, Jerry Hludzic, Bill Kelly and Carl Siracuse.

Collectively, the group had enough energy and talent to catapult them to the top. Wright produced the

Buoys' first two releases, "These Days," and their mega-hit "Timothy." Songwriter Holmes' three contributions to the Buoys album, "Timothy," "Give Up Your Guns," and "Bloodknot" were all worthy trophies - gold - silver - bronze - in the Buoys repertoire, but what was missing was a strong commitment from Scepter, a company that, after a few scant years, would cease to exist. Wright and Holmes knew that other then mandatory ads in trade magazines such as *Billboard* and *Cashbox*, there would be no promotion. If the song was not a hit The Buoys would be kicked to the side and forced to look for another label.

Buffalo's WKBW

Fate appears when least expected. In the Autumn of 1970, Scepter A&R man (Artists and Repertoire) Glen Robbins confidently walked into the office of Buffalo's Top 40 powerhouse, WKBW. Robbins' assignment was to promote Scepter artists through free records and promotional giveaways. Specifically, he was there to promote BJ Thomas' "No Love At All" (Scepter, 1971), but, surprisingly, he began to hype "Timothy," believing that it was the more commercial of the two. Robbins' approach was based on savvy marketing skills, inside contacts and a hard-to-define sixth sense.

Robbins' tactic worked beyond anything Scepter could have imagined.

"Timothy" began to receive scattered airplay in select test markets including Buffalo's WKBW, Syracuse's

WHEN, and Washington, D.C.'s WEAM. Nevertheless, the song languished nationally from lack of airplay and almost died. Finally, on January 2, 1971, it broke into the all-important *Billboard* charts. Chicago's WCFL chose the song as the "Pick Hit Of The Week." AM radio stations, quick to spot a poppy and novel tune, began placing the song into regular rotation and slowly triggered what was to become a national tsunami of chart action and controversy.

Nationally, the two-minute and 49 second record was introduced by celebrity disk jockey Cascy Kasem. "Timothy" appeared on his *American Top 40 Countdown*, as the highest debuting record for the week of April 11, 1971. That same month President Richard Nixon ended the blockade against the People's Republic of China, 200,000 anti-Vietnam War protesters marched in the shadow of the Washington Monument, Concert Promoter Bill Graham closed down Fillmore East and Fillmore West, the US Supreme Court upheld use of busing to achieve racial desegregation and killer Charles Manson was sentenced to life for the Sharon Tate murders.

"Timothy" was part of that heady cultural vortex. Ever so slowly, the song reached critical mass and then, like a nuclear chain reaction, exploded. "Timothy's" success was predicated on the amount of airplay that powerful AM stations provided. Fortunately AM radio was all over this "hot wax" phenomenon, generating hype, buzz, controversy and airplay. Airplay meant more concerts, tours, interviews and record sales.

"Timothy's" ascent was a slow, progressive one. Like an alien life form, "Timothy" demonstrated the ability to take hold, replicate and sustain itself. The song reached the *Billboard* Top 40 on April 17, 1971, remaining on the chart for eight weeks and peaking at #17. It also charted in *Cashbox* and reached #8 in *Record World*. It persevered for a remarkable 17 weeks.

The Controversy

The persistent allegations of cannibalism resulted in an urban legend, sustained by an undercurrent of rumor, innuendo and a real life mining tragedy. As more listeners began to actually listen to and understand the disturbing lyrics, "Timothy" assumed a life that went beyond the scope of a mere 45-rpm recording. Like a graveyard specter, a dark mythology began to take shape and form.

Scepter/Wand Records knew the importance of controversy. Teenage angst and corporate record sales were interconnected like high school sweethearts. "Timothy" was a well-thought-out formula that reeked of debate, pitting conservative moralists against advocates of free speech. After all, the release of "Timothy," a veiled tale about cannibalism, was certain to set off protests on both sides, as Scepter Records was well aware.

Initially, Scepter assumed a defensive stance, claiming that ol' Tim was not the third miner but actually a mule. Hoping to circumvent rumors about cannibalism, Scepter "re-surfaced" the record and issued a record sleeve of a donkey. The contrived explanation that Timothy was a mule resonated with Scepter spin-doctors, who calculated they could exploit the controversy to their advantage.

Intending to milk the controversy for all it was worth, Scepter placed ads in *Billboard* and *Cashbox Magazines* promoting a "Timothy Contest." It posed the question, "What or who was Timothy --- a boy, a mule, a dog or a canary?" More than one radio station ran their own contest asking the same distasteful question that would go unanswered in the small Schuylkill County village of Sheppton.

Sheppton Disrespect

As the bells of St. Joseph's Church pierced the air, Sheppton mourned and hoped. And prayed. Almost a decade later a song suggesting an ugly, yet possible truth, resurrected those terrible memories. Some Sheppton residents were incensed, claiming "Timothy" went too far in its graphic depiction of a coal miner's misfortune. Others argued it was mere speculation, devoid of empirically based evidence. The topic conjured primal feelings. Heated discussions ensued. It was easy to connect the dots from "Timothy" to cannibalism to Sheppton.

Schuylkill County natives voiced their personal thoughts on the matter. Aveline Stees weighed the song's purported authenticity against its metaphorical substance. She observed, "I'm not sure how I would feel if I lived in Sheppton." But, regarding those rumors of cannibalism,

Stees pondered, "It was a tragedy and perhaps the song was a bit insensitive. But then music tells it the way it is. The song implies things not in evidence but presents a very likely scenario. Perhaps, a tad hard to accept by the average person, but, indeed probable. Who knows what people might do if they are desperate enough?"

Furthermore, The Buoys, themselves, helped fuel the controversy by injecting cannibalism into the equation. In a *New York Times* article, writer Adam Di Petto wrote, "Letters from around the country are swamping Scepter Records over the hit single 'Timothy' by the Buoys. Ditty tells the story of three trapped in a mine and one of them, Timothy, is eaten by the other two. The Buoys explain that the song is a fictionalized version of a true incident that reportedly occurred many, many years ago in a Pennsylvania mine. Three were trapped in the mine, but only two came out – and bones were found." Di Petto concluded, "Whether or not Timothy is a man or a dog or a mule is the question left up in the air."

Regional on-air personalities Rich Appel, L.A. Tarone, Jay Levan, Mike Naydock and Cary D. Pall considered accusations that the song was somehow disrespectful to Sheppton villagers. All voiced similar opinions: there simply was no disrespect implied or intended.

WRNJ's Rich Appel saw no connection to the Sheppton miners. He said, "As nothing but a listener, I hear a song that tells a story that sounds fictitious, so I'm simply entertained by it. I don't feel it was meant to be disrespectful to anyone, especially since it doesn't name any names, except of course for Timothy and Joe, which I'm assuming are not names of Sheppton miners?"

Beauty, and perhaps reality, too, lies in the eye of the beholder. Jay Levan, radio personality at Schuylkill County's WPPA-AM, viewed the situation with a unique combination of experience and perspective. Concerning the cannibalism distortions and mendacities he said, "I think that any disrespect to the Coal Region in general and Sheppton in particular would be a person's perception, not the song's intention."

What really happened beneath the bowels of Sheppton was all a matter of emotionally charged conjecture. For those who dared speak the unspeakable, a modern urban legend, like a dark and evil incantation, was summoned. Sociologists used the term "contemporary legend." It became a theme that played out in Schuylkill county taprooms and roadhouses again and again, promoted by writers like Ronnie Sando, who openly spoke of the "cannibalism" allegations.

The Keystone Record Collector's B. Derek Shaw broke down the elements of the song's genesis: "The inspiration for Holmes' tune was from two other sources: the popular Tennessee Ernie Ford tune, 'Sixteen Tons' (Capitol, 1955) and the 1959 Tennessee Williams play, *Suddenly, Last Summer* which touches on cannibalism. He merged the two themes together, writing the song from a first person perspective. Jimmy Dean's "Big Bad John" (Columbia, 1961) is also a similar story.

"I doubt Holmes knew anything about the Sheppton disaster that occurred eight years prior. It was just a coincidence. Holmes, from the New York City metro area, was looking to write a song that would potentially get banned, generating more interest in The Buoys, the group that ended up recording it. That idea worked."

Shaw elaborated on his perspective regarding the musical controversy: "The song is a realistic attempt, in a first person narrative, to explain what could happen, but never coming out stating 'cannibalism.' The song borders on a psychological study when people are left in a confined area. Again Rupert Holmes never patterned the song after the Sheppton Mining Disaster," Shaw emphasized.

Bill Trousdale, President of The Pennsylvania Museum of Music and Broadcast History, stated, "I can comment from two points of view. First as a young adult at college, in Texas, I was appealed to the tune by the melodic pop and musical urgency in the music.

"The story in the lyrics was not immediately known to me. As more commentary from deejays was presented about the meaning of the song, my interest increased. I bought the tune to listen closely to the implied demise of Timothy. Upon reflection as a musicologist, the lyrics begged the question 'What would you do if you were in that situation? Could you, would you resort to cannibalism to survive?'

"This is a deeper social community discussion. When does survival trump civility? Are the rules of society null and void during a crisis? What conditions could allow such 'abhorrent' behavior.

"I could understand how the families (of Sheppton) could feel the lyrics were disrespectful. However the truth is buried in the mine, all we have is speculation, as two beliefs will continue to coexist. The question is insensitive, nonetheless the mystery, of what really happened will continue. The inquiry of speculation will continue to peak human interest as long as the truth is not known. Human nature it seems, needs but a gram of doubt, to propagate speculation, regardless of the truth," he concluded.

But Rupert Homes, who scripted the controversial tune, explained that his mindset was not about Sheppton at the time. "I was working on an arrangement of 'Sixteen Tons' for Andy Kim, and watching a cooking show on TV when the idea came to me. I thought, 'that's it,' that's the one subject no one has done a pop song about—cannibalism.' That's how the link between cannibalism and mining took place. It's not that I was out to do in mining. I mean, I respect the miners of America tremendously."

Holmes maintains that he knew nothing about the mine disaster and that his song was purely an experiment in musical fantasy. "I learned about the Sheppton Mine disaster after 'Timothy' was on the charts. If I had known about that at the time I probably never would have written the song, because I don't want to make fun of something that's tragic. I sadly found out that there actually was a parallel in reality, but only after the fact. It never occurred to me that there could be anything quite like that. It's one of those things that I wish would go away, but I have to live with it."

"Timothy" churned in the eye of the tempest. Like a spreading oil slick, the song artfully swirled and persevered. There were several distinct elements, an illogical and insane alchemy, that allowed the sustainability of this Coal Region mythology. 1971 was a time when teenagers bought 45 rpm records and listened to music on Japanese-made plastic transistor radios with alligator clips and awkward-looking earplugs. It was a time when radio was king and disc jockeys were motor-mouthed celebrities hyping the fads and trends and slogans of the day.

"Timothy" was a cultural anomaly belonging to another era. It was a retro period existing before the Internet, twitter, Facebook, i-Pods, cell phones and all the other technological devices that have redefined the teenage wasteland. The pseudo-controversy of "Timothy" would not be possible in today's cyber optic and digitized world of instantaneous communications and data collection. Also, one could argue that this fad would be quickly passed over in favor of the next sensation. Today, the song wouldn't have a chance, wouldn't have a prayer.

Florence Greenberg, head of Scepter Records, claimed she had no idea that the song was about cannibalism. Nevertheless, she enthusiastically promoted her silly and contrived "Timothy was a Mule" contest to the teenage public.

Teenagers may be emotional, unpredictable and rebellious, but they are not stupid. Most radio listeners refused to buy into Scepter's sanitized explanation. They knew that "Tim" was a man. And that he was eaten. And that Scepter was taking their money and playing them for fools.

Rupert Holmes knew it too. He said, "Scepter Records started a rumor that Timothy was a mule to try to get the taint of cannibalism out of the picture and try to make it a Top 10 record. Someone called me and said 'Was Timothy a mule? You wrote it.' And I said 'No, what can I tell you, they ate him.'"

Chapter 11
SHEPPTON MYTHOLOGY

Do the Sheppton events represent some incomprehensible influence outside our normal scope of awareness?

The term "supernatural" denotes a parallel force counter to scientific thought. In the realm of science, we connect the cause to the effect. Because of gravity the apple drops. Because of evaporation, water from earth rises, cools and returns as rain. But, with all the aforementioned weird occurrences seen in Sheppton, we are witness to only the physical manifestations. We see things, strange things, but can only guess as to the cause.

Sheppton slots congruently into this weird dynamic. Something fantastic happened in that soulless place devoid of mercy and light and forgiveness. It was a total darkness, a black hell where the ability to see movement or depth or distance was eradicated. Vision was painfully ripped away by forces more powerful than anything encountered before, and yet, even without the gift of sight, the trapped men were somehow able to see.

Humanoid figures

They existed in an illusory world, bound by invisible chains, searching for a secret chamber to shepherd them to safety. What they found was an improbable construction of majestic stairwells and humanoid figures.

They both saw bizarre things, extraordinary images that appeared in their fourteen-foot by nine-foot tomb. (Note: There have been at least five different descriptions of the confined area. Most agree that parts of the shaft were high enough for them to stand, while other sections were so low the miners had to crawl. Additionally, after continuous cave-ins, the miners were forced to locate other monkey shafts and crawl spaces, thus uncovering newer habitable sites.) Fellin and Throne saw human-like figures with lights. The miners called for light and crawled towards the figures.

Bathed in luminosity, they felt fantastically wonderful and weird at the same time. The humanoids were dressed in strange space suits with softly glowing lanterns attached to their helmets. The creatures stood on a majestic stairwell that rose higher and higher, beyond the vision of the miners.

Afterwards Fellin recollected that moment. They seemed to be in a weirdly altered condition, a dream state akin to a trip through the Knobels' Grove House of Mirrors. "The lights and figures always were in front of us," recalled Throne. "But the more we crawled toward them the further away they got. For example, I saw this man, or the dark shape of a man with a light on his helmet. I yelled, 'Show me some light over here! Over here!' Davie saw him too, but the shape of the man got smaller and smaller as we crawled toward him and then he was gone altogether."

Was it but an illusion; a stairwell never to be touched, or walked upon? Was it the stark denial of reality, an abdication of the laws of nature? Were these revelations a confabulation of a traumatized mind?

As Fellin straddled the line connecting the membrane of ecstasy to the bone of depression, his world went black. His heart was broken. The fourth day was a period of utter hopelessness and despondency. Fellin had estimated that only 75 feet of the slope had been filled with debris. The rescue team should have dug them out by now.

Nonetheless, as the sun rose that Thursday morning, hovering high above the mine, down below was a feeling of expectation. Fellin's mind drifted. He longed to work in his garden with Anna. He could almost smell the sweet taste of freshly cut grass and flowers.

Something grand was about to happen. Miraculously, the darkness turned into a scene of wonder as they both saw a doorway outlined in a "bright blue light." Fellin recalled that happening for the Philadelphia *Inquirer*: "On the fourth or fifth day, we saw this door although we had no light from above or from our helmets. The door was covered in bright blue light. It was very clear, better than sunlight. Two ordinary looking men, not miners, opened the door. We could see beautiful marble steps on the other side. We saw this for some time and then we didn't see it."

They peered into another world. Beyond the door loomed a sweeping set of marble steps that looked like an endless progression of piano keys. Dave Fellin saw an aura that shimmered with an unearthly brightness. Heaven looked back. He viewed the Golden City, a massive golden structure that seemed to stretch for miles in each direction. Angels and children played harps of bleached ivory, alabaster and gold. Fellin saw his relatives sitting in orderly groups on the steps, some near and others further away. He recognized many of them, even strangers that he instinctively sensed were related to him. Their presence made him feel protected. He heard their celestial choir, the most exquisite music he had ever heard. *When the roll is called up yonder*. He knew that soon he would be going home, carrying Throne in his arms, lifting him to his salvation, and then, in a final act of humility, would gaze into the face of God.

Perhaps it was the power of prayer and perhaps their prayers had been answered. They found comfort in the presence of Pope John XXlll, who watched them and smiled, his arms folded respectfully, a sign that they would be rescued.

Support for that blessed miracle came from curious circles. Paranormal Editor Deena West Budd offered, "Two of the most interesting out-of-body experiences I have researched occurred to the two survivors of the Sheppton Mine Disaster in 1963. Both men, in separate interviews, claimed to have spent time with a visitor during their fourteen-day ordeal, Pope John XXIII.

"In successive interviews granted with television and newspaper reporters, both men claimed to have started experiencing some amazing visions on the fourth or fifth day, although they were in total darkness. They saw a door enveloped in a bright blue light. At the door were marble stairs, and people walking up and down the steps. Beyond the door, was a garden that stretched as far as the eye could see with colorful, bright flowers and green grass. Looking down on the two miners was Pope John XXIII, although he had passed away ten weeks previously."

Budd concluded, "As both parties were interviewed separately, yet reported the same story, I tend to believe it was NOT a hallucination. I think these men were not meant to die at that time, and were visited by the spirit of Pope John XXIII to bring them the hope and strength they needed to get through those two weeks of horror."

Alignment of Planets

If one ignores spiritual and psychological explanations for inexplicable Sheppton events, perhaps an astrophysical one might suffice. Robert McGee, of the United States Mine

Rescue Association, believes there is something to learn from the alignment of the planets during major disasters.

Consulting the planets has long been a serious consideration. In earlier times, man looked to the skies for celestial messages predicting good and evil. The alignment of the planets was believed to foretell cataclysmic events, such as the end of the world or assassinations of great leaders.

Throughout history, the planets were used to guide military invasions and to plan political events. Although astrology and fortune telling were banned by Hitler's Third Reich, Wilhelm Theodor H. Wulff, a German astrologer, became Heinrich Himmler's astrologer. Himmler, one of the most powerful men in Nazi Germany, had Wulff research the anthropological and cultural history of the Aryan race, searching for mythical Nordic connections. As believers of the "Hollow Earth theory," they searched for hidden tunnels leading to earth's core.

Swiss astrologer Karl Ernst Krafft was Hitler's personal astrologer. It was Dr. Josef Goebbels, leader of the Reich Propaganda ministry, who urged Krafft to decipher the quatrains of Nosradamus to fabricate a pro-German outlook. Thousands of pamphlets were distributed with Krafft's slanted interpretation of the quatrains, assuring Germany of a victory.

Decades later, First Lady Nancy Reagan secretly consulted astrologer Joan Quigley to determine if her husband should hold press conferences, deliver speeches or journey abroad for presidential trips. Quigley claimed to have convinced President Ronald Reagan to soften his stance toward the Soviet Union. Before Reagan's 1985 Geneva summit with Soviet leader Mikhail Gorbachev, Quigley in her 1990 memoir, *What Does Joan Say?* advised Nancy Reagan that "Ronnie's 'evil empire' attitude has to go." Quigley's role became a matter of concern. The president warned his wife to be careful because it might look odd if the horoscope consultations were made public, the First Lady wrote in her 1989 memoir, *My Turn*.

Yet another text, a 1988 book by Donald Regan, former White House chief of staff, acknowledged that almost every major move the Reagans made during Regan's tenure was cleared in advance with an unknown astrologer (Joan Quigley) in San Francisco.

While some seek guidance in astrology, others have investigated the specific alignment of planets during major disasters such as Sheppton. Robert McGee explains, "I was first turned to the notion regarding the alignment of planets a few years ago after talking with an astronomical mathematician. From there I set out to examine disaster dates and the snapshots of the planets on those dates."

The researcher trusts that although planetary alignment may be a key factor in these disasters, he also investigates other variables, including human error. Says McGee: "It should be noted here that disasters such as fires and explosions are usually the result of human error and their inclusion in this discussion is suspect. Inundations of gas and water, and roof falls (cave-ins) are those worth giving any serious attention, although humans may also play a role in these as well."

He believes that planetary influence is worthy of study. McGee says, "While the contributing factors causing accidents are numerous, theorists believe the forces of these bodies on the earth may be sufficient for inclusion as a factor"

McGee, admits that the solar alignment theory is far from a pure science, but "warrants consideration." Still, he offers this caveat on the subject: "There are often numerous contributing factors leading up to events such as mine disasters. When these factors include man's stupidity and/or callous disregard of the hazards confronted, any attempt to place the blame of their cause due to the position of the planets is minimized."

Opiate receptors

Fate Magazine researcher Bill Schmeer observed, "… the cruelest blow was yet to be struck --- the blow aimed at the miners' integrity by lesser men who did not believe." The legions of non-believers and doubters caused the harm.

Not everyone placed credence in the supernatural elucidations. Critics charged that Fellin and Throne suffered the same hallucinations, at the same exact time, a malady brought on by sulfur water or the emotional stress of being interred in a pitch-black, claustrophobic coffin. There were plenty of theories and little empirical evidence on either side of the discussion.

Attempts to investigate the facts and argue each side ended, unsuccessfully. There would be little conclusion to the debate. Answers were sought. The miners were interviewed individually and together by several psychiatrists from the University of Pennsylvania, and by Dr. Richard Anderson, a medical doctor and psychiatrist from the U.S. Navy.

The authorities from the University of Pennsylvania published an article in the *American Journal of Psychiatry*. Their mixed conclusion observed that, "neither man exhibited evidence of psychosis or marked mental abnormality when examined." Even though both men had independently corroborated the other's story, their similar experiences were discounted as "delusions."

These were disrespectful words that raked across flesh like rusted barbed wire. It wasn't the endorsement they had sought. Cruelly, more harsh criticism was imminent.

After hearing Throne's recollection of bizarre creatures and stairways, some suggested that he was mentally unbalanced. Fellin and Throne eventually stopped talking about their experiences, contending that what they saw was real in spite of what anyone else thought. They were not insane. They did not hallucinate because of their life-threatening trauma. They were not addled by the effects of drinking putrid sulfur water.

While being interviewed by the *Associated Press*, Fellin argued against those theories, insisting that they were dead wrong. "Now they're trying to tell me that those things were hallucinations. That we imagined it all. We didn't! Our minds weren't playing tricks on us. I've been a hard-headed miner all my life. My mind was clear down there in the mine. These things happened! I can't explain them. I'm almost afraid to think what may be the explanation," he said.

Trapped in that dank mine pit, the miners believed their experience to be as real as was their oppressive and tangible prison. They never questioned this reality. Said Throne, "I'd sleep, I'd wake up, and I'd see all kinds of light and the actual figures of people…There were times we saw people who weren't there and lights that weren't there and doors that weren't there. Imagine seeing a regular house door down in the bottom of a mine. They now tell me these were hallucinations but the crazy thing is that Davey would see the same things I did."

At some point Fellin and Throne were forced to come to grips with the reality of being entombed in a death chamber. Slowly, they found ways to turn those 336 hours of existence into a pathway to survival. How did they do it?

The endorphins? Was that the answer? Medical researchers have known that during times of extreme stress individuals release neurotransmitters, called endorphins. These chemical agents are similar to morphine as they interact with opiate receptors in the brain to reduce our perception of pain. Endorphins also increase feelings of euphoria and modulation of appetite and allow us to experience fewer negative effects of stress.

Did the miners experience a life-saving numbness, a saving grace that helped them endure their claustrophobic hell? Did they just "shut down" in a curious tradeoff where all human emotions were killed and replaced with zombie-like numbing sensations? It might have been that simple. *Slow the heart rate and breathing until the individual is relegated to a mere organism that sucks air and pumps blood and defecates; an organism that defies the odds and miraculously survives.*

PTSD

PTSD. Post traumatic stress disorder. Shell shock. Combat fatigue. Call it what you will, but the condition remains the same.

PTSD occurs after an individual experiences a life-threatening event, or, a perceived life-threatening event. It can be in the no-man's land of South Central Los Angeles, in the streets of Mosul, Iraq, or in Afghanistan's Valley of Death. PTSD is a fear phobia. It is anticipation of yet another bomb blast, another life-threatening horrific event that we believe is going to happen. And so we wait for the next explosion, the next trauma.

As did Fellin and Throne.

Inside the dank entrails of a Sheppton coalmine with the walls threatening to cave in, they awaited death, over and over again. The unfortunates were trapped for 14 miserable, claustrophobic days, initially with little hope for food, water or rescue. Loneliness and detachment proved to be the most intolerable. One can only contemplate how David Fellin and Henry Throne dealt with the maddening terror and trauma. And no one will ever know what Louis Bova endured in his solitary chamber, after he realized that he was to die alone.

The Other Side

Although some questioned the veracity of Fellin and Throne, there were abundant reasons to accept their story as the truth. A former newspaper reporter initiated much of this.

Ed Conrad was an old school newspaperman who had worked for the Hazleton *Standard Speaker*. He was a proactive, *gonzo* journalist in the tradition of Hunter S. Thompson. Conrad imbedded himself into the story, providing an invaluable perspective. The Sheppton incident was thoroughly authenticated by Conrad who demanded that the event be considered on an academic, scientific level.

Conrad's article, "Proof of Life After Death," was published after Fellin's death in 1990. Conrad interviewed Fellin, taped the interviews, and documented Fellin's recollections in an impressive array of notarized letters. It was Conrad, singlehandedly, who investigated the Sheppton mythology, bringing the event to the attention of prominent scholars and researchers. (Note: Although Ed Conrad helped authenticate Fellin's testimony, Fellin must be given credit for initially taking steps to document his story. Fellin insisted on a psychiatric examination upon his rescue. He also offered to be polygraph tested after Bill Schmeer's 1964 *Fate Magazine* interview.)

Conrad concludes that Fellin and Throne had shared near death experiences at the same time. He continued on his mission to validate the Sheppton event. Along with Fellin, they went to Headwaters, Virginia, where Fellin was interviewed by the late Dr. Elizabeth Kubler-Ross. The Swiss psychiatrist authored numerous books on death, including *On Death and Dying* (1969), which detailed the stages in understanding the death process. Conrad and Fellin affirmed that Kubler-Ross believed the miners' experience was evidence that life after death does exist. Kubler-Ross remarked on the resilience demonstrated by the miners, after five days of entombment. She called their behavior "a guideline for our miners, soldiers, mountain climbers and all those at risk to face a similar ordeal one day."

Additional support came from Dr. Bruce Greyson, a psychiatrist at the University of Connecticut Health Center and editor for *The Journal of Near-Death Studies*. Greyson, citing the simultaneous paranormal experiences, said: "If they can corroborate each other's account, they could provide evidence for the realty of 'The Other Side' beyond anything yet available."

Those were the words Fellin and Conrad needed to hear --- an affirmation and validation of the Sheppton miracle.

Nevertheless, what he confessed to Conrad would prove to be the most bizarre in lyric and tone. Fellin spoke of out-of-body occurrences, time travel and contact with both Pope John XXIII and humanoid creatures. One of the last testaments divulged to Conrad would be the most profound. He had ability, clairvoyance. Fellin said he knew things, saw things. He confided, "There are more planets with human life in the universe then there are grains of sand on all the beaches of the world."

There was more to be revealed. The miners said that they underwent an out-of-body episode. They rose above the mine and looked down upon hundreds of rescue workers and support personnel. Fellin told a Lancaster reporter that he was able to fly through the mountain of debris and rocket skyward, breaking out of the mine and landing on firm earth to the sound of cheering Sheppton residents. He rushed into the loving arms of Anna. Fellin experienced this out of body astral projection numerous times while Throne admitted that he was able to do it once.

Years later, after innumerable privately tape recorded interviews, as well as, public meetings, the miners held to their story of visitations by bizarrely outfitted men and stairwells of white marble.

It is important to understand that Fellin did not approach the media to discuss his ordeal, but was only responding to their voracious requests for interviews. He did not initiate these interviews and it would be unfair to characterize him as a publicity seeker. And, too, as Anna instructed her husband to not cooperate with the media, Fellin, in turn, instructed Throne to resist these potential traps --- something that the younger miner failed to heed.

Fellin fiercely defended his recollection that the presence of John XXIII saved them, providing the faith and resilience to endure until their moment of rescue. Fellin and Throne did not care if people thought they were crazy. They had heard worse. They knew what they had experienced. They held to that belief.

Martin Piechota believed that the mysterious Men in Black, emissaries from beyond, visited Sheppton. According to folklore, the MIB make contact with human beings who have witnessed UFO sightings. Piechota regarded Sheppton as a "less known, religious event" with parallels to the 1917 Miracle at Fatima.

Finally, Daniel Rolph, writing for the Historical Society of Pennsylvania, observed that the ultimate deduction may lie, not in the debate between miracles and hallucinations, but in the eye of the observer. His "Mines: Mysterious Discoveries & Miracles" intoned: "The story of Throne and Fellin's survival and rescue was enough to captivate the world's attention, but *it was what they claimed they saw and heard*, while entombed, that fascinated the public, statements which both men swore as to their authenticity, both separately and publicly, emphatic declarations which they took to their graves, though others believed they had simultaneously witnessed the same hallucinations."

During an interview with the Philadelphia *Inquirer*, Fellin attempted to explain the bizarre visions seen in the mine. Of the stairwells and humanoid creatures, he recounted: "We saw many other things like that, that you couldn't explain. But I'm not going to tell you about them because I feel too deeply about all this."

Dave Fellin was 85-years-old at the time of his death. He had died 27 years after his rescue. Fellin had been generously forthcoming and candid with his personal disclosures. Nevertheless, there was something that he was holding back, something he declined to examine. "I'm not going to tell you about them," were his cryptic words, perhaps the biggest clue of all. Clearly, there were vile things that he refused to discuss and things that will never be revealed. The secret Fellin guarded could have unlocked the mystery of Sheppton, could have granted the sweet salvation of closure. But it was a revelation Dave Fellin purposively took to the grave.

Chapter 12
VILLAGE PARIAH

David Fellin possessed a miner's instinct, an intuition that one could sense but not quite put a finger on. He was able to look people in the eye, read their body language like the morning paper and immediately size them up. In a nanosecond he knew friend from foe, safety from danger. There wasn't a scientific or sociological name for it, but he had it.

Perhaps he was psychic. Fellin saw things others could not. He said that he experienced things of a preternatural nature.

He was also superstitious.

Fresh White Oak

Fellin's faith was a curious intermingling of the sacred and the supernatural. He was steeped in pragmatism, dogma and the philosophies of Mahatma Gandhi and others. As a member of St. Joseph's Roman Catholic Church, Fellin believed that the Grace of God would protect him. During that horrifying two-week period, both Fellin and Throne prayed several times each day, asking for rescue. It became their new religion: tap, dig, listen and pray.

Remarkably, Fellin's superstitious nature played a role in the rescue attempt. An interesting, provocative article titled "Oak Mine Timbers," documented the superstitious Fellin and detailed how his odd behavior impeded the rescue attempt.

The August 25, 1963, UPI dispatch from Sheppton, PA to the Providence *Sunday Journal*, as written by reporter George Monteiro, revealed:

"An old miner's superstition that freshly cut oak is better than old, delayed rescue operations here for a brief time. When rescuers told David Fellin that timber was being sent down so the men could shore up their tiny chamber, he replied: 'I want white oak, fresh cut from the bush.' Work was halted at the surface while men went into the surrounding woods to cut oak.

"Clyde MacHamer, president of the Independent Miners and Associates, said rescuers had plenty of two-day-old oak on hand but had to bow to Mr. Fellin's superstition. 'He's an old miner,' MacHamer said, 'and just wanted to smell fresh-cut oak.'"

When it came down to it the old miner was a complicated man, an unlikely hero who, confronted by harsh circumstances, responded in kind. He was steady, controlled, but also unpredictable. Many described Fellin as "honorable," "kind hearted" and a friend of the miners. They were continually mistreated. Working like dogs, they were ordered to crawl into the depths of hell, and were blamed for everything that went wrong.

The miners were easy, convenient targets. James Hyslop, president of the Hanna Coal Company, was among the denigrators. In 1952 he declared that the majority of mining accidents were preventable and caused by the miners themselves, "There are on an average 1,000 men who lose their lives in the coal mines annually," Hyslop said. "Ninety percent of the men lose their lives in the ordinary accidents, accidents in which the individual plays an important role usually."

Fellin didn't agree with any of that. He knew that the companies were largely responsible for deaths, caused by unsafe working conditions. Some 32,000 men and boys had been killed or injured between 1869 and 1916, one of mining's most dangerous periods. Breaker boys, not even in their teens, had worked the most hazardous jobs, making less than ten cents an hour. At one time, miners worked 14-hour shifts, entering the mines before sunrise and climbing out after sunset. They existed in darkness, human moles who never felt the warmth of the sun.

Fellin continued to speak out against corporate injustice and incompetence, and champion the rights of the miners. But what goes around, comes around. His spontaneity and unhindered candor would come back to haunt him.

Magnetic pull

Sheppton emitted a magnetic pull. Like a trapdoor spider, it drew curious individuals into its web and mysteriously affected their behavior. One such individual, in the guise of Marine Corps physician Captain James Roland, sported government-issued khakis and wore a polished stethoscope around his neck. During the rescue operations the Captain issued daily news updates to the salivating media and passed out free energy wafers to spectators.

Sharon Drebitko-Kolenick, Andrew Drebitko's daughter, told reporters that the "Doctor" handed out free energy pills to the rescuers. But 23-year-old Roland, who claimed to be from Rosemont, Pennsylvania, was found to be an imposter, possibly a Philadelphia-area college student. Basking in false celebrity, he furtively disappeared before he could be apprehended and possibly arrested. His true identity was never revealed.

There were others, too, individuals who should have acted honorably and courageously during the Sheppton disaster, but instead pandered to the lowest of denominators. The United Mine Worker's of America (UMWA) President W. A. "Tony" Boyle was of that ilk. After all the dust had settled, Boyle proved to be a liar and much worse.

Boyle was an instigator of the vilest kind. He accused H. Beecher Charmbury, Secretary of Mines and Mineral Industries, of sabotaging the rescue by refusing to believe the miners were still alive. Boyle charged that rescue operations did not begin until after the fifth day of entombment. Not missing a step, a boastful Tony Boyle gave full credit to his UMWA for initiating the rescue attempt. He bragged: "It became increasingly apparent that not much was being done in a constructive way to a effect the rescue of these men.

"Upon hearing these allegations, the District Seven office with my approval sent representatives to the scene of the disaster to do everything possible to effectuate a rescue operation. At the insistence of our representatives, it was decided to start borehole drilling operations because this appeared to be the only way of bringing these men out of the mine alive. I am pleased here today that these efforts appear to be bearing fruit and we hope they will eventually result in a successful rescue..."

That pompous dissertation was merely the opening salvo of Boyle's tainted legacy.

Elected president of the UMWA in 1963, Boyle had his presidency immediately rocked with turmoil and strife. After winning a close, hotly contested, election against Joseph A. Yablonski, Boyle was accused of rigging the voting results.

One month later, Yablonski, his wife, Margaret, and daughter, Charlotte, were found murdered in their home. Boyle was immediately suspected of the crime, and in 1974 found guilty of three 1st degree murder convictions. He was sentenced to life imprisonment for the revenge killings, and, although there was justice and closure, there was also sadness that settled over the Coal Region.

Public opinion

Nevertheless, there seemed at least one genuine hero of whom the Coal Region could be proud. After the rescue, the patches were drunk with celebration. Davie Fellin's courage and heroism were toasted with applause and rounds of free drinks at local taverns like Dado's Cafe. It was a Coal Region celebration for one of their own.

Sadly, the celebration was short lived. Public opinion instantly changed after Fellin's reputation of honesty and courage sank into disrepute.

During a news conference, one of numerous retellings of his Sheppton ordeal, Fellin charged that after the fifth day of entombment he had given up hope. Despondency overcame him and his tough, usually-positive attitude was dramatically tested. He believed that the rescue team had forgotten them and wondered if they would ever be rescued. Of that revelation, Fellin confessed, "When I thought someone had let me down, I felt worse. I couldn't hear the drill and I thought we should have been out by then."

Fellin's remarks came across as crass and inconsiderate. He violated the basic, most sacrosanct rule of any civilized people. He disrespected the men whose bravery had plucked him from the bowels of the mineshaft, granting his freedom. One of the popular sayings in the patches was, "Don't bite the hand that feeds you." Fellin had heard it before, had probably spoken it, too. But, on this occasion, he callously slandered its meaning. That kind of disrespect scored no points in the Coal Region.

Clyde Machamer, President of the Independent Mine Workers Association, was caught by surprise at Fellin's insensitive comments. In light of the tremendous amount of rescue work, materials and manpower that the IMWA had provided, Machamer was quick to level his own criticism. He said: "The man should be entirely grateful, I should think, for the tremendous rescue operation that was carried on here. It's sort of a derogatory statement to make on the work done by the rescue workers. I can't comprehend why such a statement was made."

Even Fellin's co-partner Gene Gibbons attempted to diffuse the situation and explain Fellin's mindset and lack of knowledge about the rescue attempt. "Fellin is speaking without having all the facts and in a tired, weakened condition. I think I am better qualified at this point with all the facts at hand to speak for the partnership and I want to repeat again my words of praise for all who helped in the rescue effort. I have not been permitted to see (Fellin) and tell him of the stupendous effort made to save him," Gibbons clarified.

Secretary Charmbury also expressed concern about Fellin's poorly chosen words. "If that's Fellins's feelings, he's perfectly free to feel any way he wants. I know Fellin's statement could possibly hurt the morale of some of the volunteer workers who have been coming here. I'm sure Fellin isn't aware of the conditions that existed at the slope. I'm not going to be drawn into any controversy with Fellin or anybody else." Charmbury emphasized that the pressing matter at hand was "to get Bova out."

The easy going Dave Fellin stopped smiling. There were no more jokes. He averted his eyes. The world watched as the miner changed from working class hero to hapless punching bag. He became the proverbial scapegoat, the village pariah.

Some murmured, "It could only happen in the Coal Region," a truism not far removed from reality, and, another example of the region's odd incongruity.

Chapter 13
HOLLOW EARTH

The candid descriptions presented by Dave Fellin and Hank Throne parallel what has been described as the "Hollow Earth Theory," a strange belief proclaiming that humanoid creatures dwell within the earth's core.

Frequently in recorded history, accounts of civilizations residing within a hollow Earth have assumed a role in numerous creation myths. Much like Fortean lore, ufology and explorations into the supernatural, the hollow Earth theory has created a cultish fascination for the unknown. The theory boasts a long list of proponents and an astounding connection to Sheppton.

The theory originated in a 1692 scientific paper by Edmund Halley (of Halley's Comet fame) and affirmed that Earth consisted of a shell about 800 km thick, with two inner concentric shells and an innermost core with the same approximate diameter as the planet Mars. Halley believed that the inner earth could be inhabited. Later, in the seventeenth century, Leonhard Euler contributed to the theory. He proposed that a single-shell hollow earth contained a small sun that provided light and warmth for an inhabited civilization

In 1818 John Cleves Symmes furthered the radical idea of a hollow earth. A private expedition of two sailing vessels, the *Seraph* and the *Annawan*, was readied to embark on a mission to locate the holes leading to earth's core. Although newly elected President Andrew Jackson halted the mission, interest in other exploratory ventures remained.

The parameters of the hollow Earth theory began to take shape. Others stepped forward to propagate the unorthodox hypothesis. *The Hollow Globe*, published in 1868 by professor W.F. Lyons, articulated another hollow Earth premise. Marshall Gardner's *A Journey to the Earth's Interior* (1913) proposed that an interior sun radiated within the Earth. Gardner built a working model of his hollow earth and patented it. And in 1964, Rosicrucian leader Raymond W. Bernard published *The Hollow Earth – the Greatest Geographical Discovery in History Made by Admiral Richard E. Byrd in the Mysterious Land Beyond the Poles – the True Origin of the Flying Saucers.*

Halley's theory is not relegated to, or solely of a product of past history. In more recent times, Utah Elders Steve Curry and Rodney M. Cluff organized a 2005 expedition to go to the North Pole with faithful Mormons and explore the interior of the Earth. According to a survey done by R. Clayton Brough, four percent of the Latter Day Saints population believe that the hollow Earth theory is a probable explanation for the location of the lost 10 tribes of Israel. Curry chartered the Russian nuclear icebreaker *YAMAL* with a capacity for 108 passengers. After Curry died in 2006, Brooks A. Agnew vowed to take 100 scientists and film makers to the Artic opening. The ill-fated expedition, in search of the lost Israelites who inhabit the earth's interior, unfortunately, was never realized.

Cluff, author of *World Top Secret: Our Earth is Hollow* (2014), investigated the theory for years. He initially contacted Curry to organize the North Pole expedition. "I firmly believe there is a substantial amount of scientific, historical and scriptural evidence to support the theory," he said. Cluff believed the inner earth opening was marked by land about five degrees from the pole.

When asked about the Sheppton incident, Cluff immediately made the connection. Cluff told this author, "Well, yes, it is all related. Many times when people are near death, they see spirit beings from the spirit world around us." As Rodney Cluff explained, "Our earth is alive, a living being. It has a spirit that gives it life, just like our spirit gives us life. The spirits of all people when they die, go to the spirit world of this earth to continue their existence."

Cluff, a prominent hollow Earth theorist, is certain that paradise exists as an inner sun radiating inside Earth. He says, "The spirit world is divided into two parts, paradise and hell, which are separated by a great gulf of space. The location of paradise in the physical world is the inner sun. Hell is the shell of the planet. The great gulf that separates them is the hollow in the earth." Some have suggested that the vision of Pope John XXIII seen by Fellin and Throne may have been an example of Cluff's spirit world energy and a further example of life after death.

Richard Sharpe Shaver

John Cleves Symmes is recognized as the most famous of the early hollow earth advocates. Decades later, Richard Sharpe Shaver, a Berwick, PA, native, resurrected that hypothesis for a curious modern day audience.

It all began after Shaver wrote a controversial letter to *Amazing Stories* magazine editor Ray Palmer, who helped co-create a cultish fad. At the age of seven, a violent accident shattered Palmer's spine. His growth was stunted, and his deformity begat a lifetime of health-related issues and a reclusive, almost paranoid, existence. As a coping mechanism, Palmer entered into the fantastic world of 1930s science fiction, worlds created not of hard science and advanced technology, but of imagination and possibility. It was a world of pulp fiction, an era before man walked upon the moon and before over one thousand communications and spy satellites cluttered the skies.

Shaver's letter caught Palmer's attention. Shaver wrote that he had been the guest of what remained of a giant race called the Elder Race, or Titans, an underground civilization inhabiting caverns under the earth. Shaver revealed that, while working as a welder in a car factory, he heard voices transmitted through his welding gun. Shaver listened to mentally deranged Deros, degenerate descendants of an advanced alien race, who kidnapped and sexually tortured humans. They ate the flesh of others.

Richard Shaver became an unlikely icon. He claimed that he had been held prisoner by the Deros, and tortured by their "damnable rays." Editor Ray Palmer published the letters between 1945 and 1948, and instructed his sci-fi readers that the stories, known as "The Shaver Mysteries," were authentic. Palmer aggressively promoted Shaver's letters as true accounts of ancient subterranean civilizations.

Shaver's account was unsubstantiated, yet interesting and provocative. The hollow Earth theory was popular in pre-science times, before scientists were able to identify Earth's outer and inner core and understand the structure of Earth's mantle. However, geologists left little doubt that the hollow Earth theory simply had no validity, as earth's core contains a mass of extremely hot magma, a molten and semi-molten rock mixture spewing off toxic gases.

Still, in the 1940s, people hungered for Shaver's fantastic story of an advanced underground civilization. He sold his goods, and they were bought ten times over by a public who demanded more. The Shaver Mysteries became a national phenomenon, providing positive distraction for a war-weary public. Shaver Mystery Club societies were created in several cities. Readership of *Amazing Stories* increased in monthly circulation from about 135,000 to 185,000.

Although unique for the period, Shaver borrowed heavily from H.G. Wells' *Time Machine* and H.P. Lovecraft's Cthulhu mythos. Shaver's contributions, welcomed as novel and profound, resonated between confirmation and debate. As the controversy continued for decades, some questioned if Shaver's tale was science fiction or sciencefact. Many believed him. Shaver always averred that his story was true, although the location of the entrance to this underground world of Titans and Deros was never revealed.

Unfortunately, other individuals, such as self-proclaimed scientist F. Amadeo Giannini, introduced a morass of fabrication and lies into the hollow Earth debate.

In his *Worlds Beyond the Poles; Physical Continuity of the Universe*, (1959), Giannini, described the so-called secret diary of Admiral Byrd. The diary was dated February 19, 1947 and titled *The Inner Earth - My Secret Diary*. In 1926, American explorer Admiral Richard Byrd flew from the Norwegian Arctic island of Spitsbergen in an attempt to be the first to fly to the North Pole. Byrd received the Medal of Honor for his accomplishments.

But over thirty years later, Byrd's alleged "secret" diary revealed unknown civilizations deep within the Earth's interior. According to Byrd's "diary," the explorer discovered an unknown civilization and was welcomed by its technologically advanced inhabitants during his exploratory flight over the North Pole. Byrd purportedly wrote of entering the hollow interior of the earth and traveling 17 miles over mountains, lakes, rivers and green vegetation. He saw tremendous animals resembling prehistoric mammoths and was welcomed into a thriving, higher civilization called Agartha. The external temperature was 74 degrees Fahrenheit, heated by a sun below the Earth. Byrd wrote that the North and South Poles are only two of many openings into the center of the Earth.

Giannini's hoax immaturely plagiarized Admiral's Byrd's actual account of his 1926 North Pole flight, with numerous scientific inaccuracies. Giannini then dismissively inserted theatrical quotes from the MGM motion picture *Lost Horizon*. Blending science with fantasy Giannini copied earlier themes from fiction by Edgar Rice Burroughs and Jules Verne, all wrapped in a deceptive cloak. His scheme was immediately found out.

Casting F. Amadeo Giannini's trickery aside, we can see that there appears to be something more substantial and concrete to the story.

The Watcher Files

Hollow Earth advocates have cited Sheppton-like incidents in numerous accounts. Ronald A. Calais, writing in the *Newsletter for The Committee For the Scientific Evaluation of PSI*, provided an account of a laborer in Staffordshire, England, who discovered a cave with a stone staircase leading into a vast cavern filled with strange machinery of an alien civilization. Author Eric Norman in his book *The Under-People: the startling discovery of a lost world*, offered accounts of alien men and majestic stairways. Norman observed the recurrent theme reflected in the visionary experience of David Fellin and Henry Throne, "who told of seeing a large door in the rock wall that was illuminated by a blue light. The two miners claim to have watched the door open and seen a group of strange men dressed in 'weird outfits' standing on a beautiful marble stairway." Similar sightings have been reported in various parts of the world, making Sheppton an anomaly within a larger anomaly. Whatever this bizarre blue light and strange humanoid – connection may prove to be, it exists beyond the boundaries of the Coal Region.

Sheppton was not alone in tales of hollow-Earth weirdness. Evidence of subterranean civilizations, stairwells and non-human creatures can be found throughout history, according to devotees of The Watcher Files. This group, part of a collective of scholars of paranormal phenomena, promotes hollow Earth theories of government conspiracies, hidden UFO bases, and alien civilizations. The Watcher Files scripted the following account that included an interesting Sheppton correlation. The account read:

"Interviews with survivors of a mine explosion in December 26,1945, known as the 'Belva Mine Disaster,' appeared in the December 1981 - January 1982 issues of newspapers in Pineville, Kentucky and elsewhere. The interviews revealed that some of the trapped men saw a 'door' in one of the walls open, and a man dressed like a 'lumberjack' emerged from a well-lighted room. After assuring the men that they would be rescued, the strange visitor returned to the room and closed the door. These 'lumberjack-like' entities have been described by miners in other parts of the country and in other nations as well. There seems to be some confusion as to whether they are physical or Para physical entities.

"A somewhat similar incident allegedly took place several years ago near (Sheppton), Pennsylvania," The Watcher Files continued. They observed: "Of the three victims of this particular mine disaster, only two were rescued. However both described a similar Para physical encounter with strange 'men' who entered the caverns and gave light to the two trapped miners and told them that they would be rescued. They (the miners) were uncertain whether the entities were humans or supernatural beings, however, much of their collective 'hallucination' contained both physical as well as supernatural elements. The bluish 'light' which illuminated the room, they said, was real, but other holographic-like visuals that appeared on the walls, when touched by their hands, either disappeared or revealed solid rock behind."

After the one-year anniversary of the Sheppton disaster, Bill Schmeer, program director at Hazleton's WAZL radio station, contacted Fellin and Throne. Schmeer stated that his intention was not to explain the phenomena, but only to report it for *Fate Magazine*. He referred to the miner's "continuous, collective hallucinations."

Dave Fellin confided to Schmeer that he saw three non-human creatures in the mine. Fellin described them as "ruggedly handsome, about six feet, three inches tall, with bronze-colored skin and very slightly pointed ears." They had athletic builds, like "football players." Fellin said they had thin lips and "normal eyes." They wore a wide head-band, open at the top, to reveal dark, straight hair.

Interviewed separately, Throne's recollection of the humanoids offered a variation of the theme. The visitors had high cheekbones, Caucasian eyes and thin lips, he said. Their skin was darker on the hands and toes than on their faces. Their hair was ear-length, combed back at the top but falling on the sides. The three wore green-gray garments similar to Japanese *kimonos*. They had open-sandals on their feet. Bill Schmeer provided a fitting epitaph of the supernatural event, observing that *Fate Magazine* described Sheppton as "unmatched in the annals of psychic research."

Ongoing Insanity

Researcher Martin Piechota attributed the Sheppton visitation to the mysterious Men in Black. He cited the three humanoids observed by Fellin and Throne as proof of this visitation. The 16-inch by 24-inch blue, triangular plaque was a sacrament they offered to the miners. Piechota held that the heart-shaped plaque represented eventual rescue.

Like lava flowing down a mountainside, the Sheppton mythology persisted. It became an ongoing insanity, the telling and retelling of Sheppton entering into the realm of the bizarre. As inexplicable as these images were, some believed they were not unique to Sheppton but part of a larger paradigm. Examples have been cited, identifying similar accounts of mysterious stairwells and underground dwellers, with the name of Richard Sharpe Shaver being often mentioned.

The relationship between Ray Palmer and Richard Shaver was joined at the intersection between insanity and delusion, between crass exploitation and naivete. To that end, Palmer was more adept at self-promotion than in maintaining confidentiality. In keeping with his win-at-all-costs-mentality, Palmer publicly revealed that his friend Richard Shaver was mentally ill. He said that Shaver spent eight years, not in the Cavern World as a prisoner of the Deros, but in a mental ward at Michigan's Ypsilanti State Hospital. While there, Shaver was treated for an undetermined psychosis, most likely paranoid schizophrenia.

Shaver responded to Palmer's expose, but adhering to his bizarre story about the hollow earth, he addressed the accusations of his mental health. He wrote, "My problems, I realized, did not stem from some kind of mental impairment. I wasn't crazy in the traditional sense, even though at times I felt like I was being driven mad by the hateful rays that were being beamed at me by the people below. No, I was sane in an insane world.

"I have always wondered," Shaver continued, "how many people, who have been institutionalized because they were diagnosed as crazy, were in fact victims, such as myself, of the damnable rays. Did they themselves think that they were insane because of the voices they heard in their heads and voluntarily committed themselves? Even today I still wonder if most forms of mental illness are not actually insidious attacks from the world below."

Yes, Richard Sharpe Shaver demonstrated classic symptoms of paranoid schizophrenia, but although he was mentally ill, he was also somewhat of a genius. His delusions were implausibly accepted and believed by many. By giving birth to the present-day cult version of the hollow Earth theory, Shaver added to the fabric of Coal Region mythology, thematically and forever linked to Sheppton.

Chapter 14
THE GOOD POPE

Bathed in vestiges of courage and survival, the Sheppton rescue similarly exuded an aura of the miraculous. Some were convinced that what had transpired in that horrible pit was nothing short of a miracle, evidence of the workings of God.

David Fellin said that the presence of Pope John XXlll, historically one of the most popular of the popes, played an important role in his capacity to survive. Explaining the purported papal visitation, Fellin told one reporter: "He was always a little bit to the rear on my right side and stayed with us all the time."

The Pope materialized and remained with the miners until their extrication from the mineshaft. Even stranger was the fact that the benevolent Pope had died two months prior to the Sheppton disaster. Pope John XXIII perished in the ornate chambers of the Vatican Palace. His death, at age 81, was caused by peritonitis brought on by a stomach tumor. The date was June 3rd, 1963.

John XXIII's death occurred after the Second Vatican Council's first session, four-and-a-half years following his election. Pope Paul VI, who reigned until 1978, succeeded him. The new pontiff, perhaps as an acknowledgement to John XXIII, broke with tradition as he admitted five women as delegates to Vatican II.

According to writer Nora V. Clemente-Arnaldo, because of the timing of the pope's death, the Sheppton incident was fervently viewed as another of John's miracles, one that saved the two miners. She wrote, "Like St. John Vianney, Pope John XXIII is also credited with after-death appearances. The story written by Madeline Pecora Nugent in the *"Messenger of St. Anthony,"* gives the documented testimony of two coal miners, David Fellini [sic] and Henry Throne, trapped 300 feet underground in Pennsylvania way back in August 1963, 10 weeks after the death of Pope John XXIII. This is what the two said: *'That they both saw the 'Good Pope' in his black cassock grinning comfortingly and lovingly at them in the chamber, while his body radiated the bluish light. That he was with them until their successful miraculous rescue on 27 August 1963.'*

"Clearly, the Lord answered Pope John XXIII's prayer by saving from death these two trapped miners given up for dead," Clemente-Arnaldo concluded of the Coal Region after -death saga.

Angelo Giuseppe Roncalli

Angelo Giuseppe Roncalli (1881-1963) was elected Pope at the age of 77. Upon his election, Roncalli was the first Pope in more than 500 years to take the pontifical name of "John." As St. John XXIII, he led the Roman Catholic Church from October 28, 1958, to his death in 1963. Although it was a comparatively brief five-year reign, it flowered with mandates that touched the lives of the common person.

John was more accessible than his predecessors. He left the Vatican to meet his flock, visiting polio-afflicted children in hospitals and inmates in Rome's Regina Coeli prison. Because of his simple, pastoral style, he came to be known affectionately as the "Good Pope."

He frequently attended parishes in Rome and was known to stroll around the city, alone, during the night, hence the whispered and cryptic name, "Johnny Walker." True believers contend that the purported Sheppton visitation was in character with Pope John's assertiveness and personal style.

Initially assumed to wear the cloak of a mere "caretaker" pope, he surprised many with his vision and activism. John was viewed as a hero to liberal Catholics for having convened the Second Vatican Council (1962-1965) to help the Church confront change and challenge in the world. The Second Vatican Council brought the church into the modern era and allowed Mass to be celebrated in local languages rather that in Latin.

It also encouraged greater dialogue with those who worshipped other faiths, especially Jews. He championed openness to non-Catholic Christians and to the modern world. John's concern was for the world and for all humankind rather than solely for the Church. His most famous statement was, "We were all made in God's image, and thus, we are all Godly alike."

John XXIII's Encyclical on Establishing Universal Peace in Truth, Justice, Charity, and Liberty, as presented on April 11, 1963, impacted the Civil Rights Movement of the 1960s, as well as, human rights. It read in part: "Today, on the contrary, the conviction is widespread that all men are equal in natural dignity; and so, on the doctrinal and theoretical level, at least, no form of approval is being given to racial discrimination. All this is of supreme significance for the formation of a human society animated by the principles we have mentioned above, for man's awareness of his rights must inevitably lead him to the recognition of his duties. The possession of rights involves the duty of implementing those rights, for they are the expression of a man's personal dignity. And the possession of rights also involves their recognition and respect by other people."

Dave Fellin knew that John XXIII was different. He was drawn to the idea of the Pope calling for the Second Vatican Council and challenging church tradition. John took the dialogue a step further. His major encyclical, *Pacem in Terris* ("Peace on Earth"), was an essay that outlined in human terms the requirements for world peace.

It was positive and hopeful. He said that for humankind's survival, it was essential to construct a peaceful coexistence. It was important for Capitalists to speak with Marxists and to differentiate between political ideology and actual governments.

Dave Fellin had a good feeling about this. John wanted to thaw the Cold War and begin a conversation with the Communists. It sounded unthinkable at the time, but Pope John desired to talk to Comrade Khrushchev and the Communist Party. Everyone else ran from them or feared them, but the Pope said we should treat them as equals. It was believed that John had personally intervened during the 1962 Cuban missile crisis, encouraging the United States, the Soviet Union and Cuba to exercise caution and restraint. Fellin had every reason to be optimistic about The Good Pope.

Mystic events

Based on his merits of opening the Second Vatican Council, reigning Pope Francis declared John XXIII a saint on July 5, 2013. Although there appeared to have been at least two other authenticated miracles (including Sheppton) Francis opted to waive the requisite second miracle usually needed for non-martyrs to reach sainthood.

Nevertheless, several documented mystic events attributed to John XXIII were acknowledged as true miracles. These included the 1966 documented case of Sister Caterina Capitani, a nun from the Naples region, who suffered multiple stomach ulcers and other grave intestinal maladies. Another took place in Sicily in 1967. It concerned a woman who suffered from tubercular peritonitis and a cardiac problem. Both individuals were cured after experiencing a mystical visitation by the Good Pope.

Barbie Latza Nadeau reported that a nun who witnessed John XXIII's divine intercession, was present at the St. Peter's Square canonization. She observed, "John XXIII's solitary miracle worker will be a Sister Adele Labianca, the nun who witnessed the inexplicable healing of Sister Caterina Capitani, a Neapolitan nun who had endured 14 surgeries for a gastric hemorrhage. The sick sister was healed after relics from John XXIII were placed on the fistula on her abdomen.

"After that, Sister Caterina apparently saw a vision of John XXIII in her sickroom as she lay dying, and the papal ghost told her to get up, that she was healed. 'I'm hungry, I want to eat,' she kept on saying, despite the fact that all she ate would just come out of the fistula in her abdomen. She carried on saying: Pope John told me, the wound is healed,' Sister Adele explained... Multiple doctors agreed that there was no medical explanation of her healing. She died in 2010 of natural causes."

Dual canonization

A dual canonization was held at the Vatican on April 27, 2014. John XXIII and John Paul II were made saints because of their palpable holiness, and because they were both considered responsible for medical miracles.

John's canonization was viewed by the masses. They came in droves, seeking healing and mercy, assuming a personal walk of faith. They paid homage to his humanitarian legacy and prayed to a piece of his exhumed flesh. The three *"miracles"* included Sister Adele Labianca, who had witnessed John XXIII's miracle.

The canonization of Pope John XXIII contributed to a renewed interest in the rescue of Fellin and Throne after several Vatican scholars cited Sheppton as a probable miracle performed by John. On a EWTN (Eternal Word Television Network) coverage of John XXIII's 2014 canonization, Franciscan Missionary Rev. Fr. Joseph Mary stated that "they (Fellin and Throne) both witnessed the appearance of Pope John XXIII, who had just died 10 weeks prior and he was much younger, about half the age of which he died at 81, dressed in a black cassock, with his arms crossed and smiling." Of this, Fr. Joseph Mary observed, "We are a part of the communion of the saints."

Mine Miracle

But there was much more to this man than simple miner's superstition. Several individuals, men of the cloth, intervened during Fellin's most challenging time. Father Svercheck, the Fellins' parish priest, was constantly offering comfort and prayers to Anna Fellin and her family. He offered her the gift of hope.

A Roman Catholic missionary, Rev. Edmond Roman, brought holy medals to the site. The religious items, blessed by Pope Paul VI, were donated by a Hazleton family who had just returned from a Vatican trip. Rev. Roman lowered a rosary, two St. Christopher's medals through the six-inch borehole that became both a corporal and spiritual lifeline.

Inside the tomb, Fellin had no realization of events occurring above the ground. Like many families, the Fellin clan harbored their share of conflict. Dave hadn't spoke with his brother Joe for nearly 20 years. But it was Joe Fellin, in the spirit of atonement, who demanded that a rescue attempt be made. And it was Joe, who walked directly to the site and placed his foot on a spot and instructed, "Drill the hole here." Joe Fellin became one of Sheppton's true heroes, in every sense of the word, and was responsible for their eventual rescue.

The miracle of Sheppton was the lead story in newspapers across America. The implication that a miracle occurred 330 feet below the ground was oft repeated, citing the miner's vision of Pope John XXIII. Against all odds, the trapped miners had been liberated via a rescue technique never before attempted. *The Los Angeles Times* published a front-page story bearing the headline, "MINE MIRACLE."

During their entombment the miners perceived strange apparitions. Those hours trapped in the cold, dark pit allowed them time to question what was real and what was not. They survived, day by day, praying for an improbable rescue. They both knew that if they gave up, they would go stark raving mad, would act out their insanity in the pit and would most likely kill each other. Still, they pondered their existential reality. Every day Fellin challenged Pope John, pleading, "I demand to know. What have I done to deserve this torment and punishment?"

The image of John XXlll intermingled with other unexplainable visions. Some alleged they were part of another interconnected dimension. Fellin thought that the white marble stairway, filled with a bluish luminance, led out of the mine and to the Gates of Heaven. He described family members who sat on the stairway, praying, encouraging the miners to climb their way to freedom.

According to writer Martin Piechota, "Three men appeared to Fellin and Throne with a plaque. The men were six-feet three-inches tall, with bronze-colored skin and slightly pointed ears. They were dressed in green-gray garments with open sandals on their feet.

"One of the characters in the apparition seen by the two miners was carrying a tablet or slate that had no writing on it. This may have been a symbolic message that Pope John XXlll had died... The present Pope, John Paul II, revealed the secret. It predicted the assassination attempt on his life."

(Note: John Paul II was shot four times and wounded by Mehmet Ali Ağca while he was entering St. Peter's Square at Vatican City. The assassination attempt took place on Wednesday, 13 May 1981. Ağca was apprehended immediately and sentenced to life in prison by an Italian court. The Pope later forgave Ağca, who was pardoned by

Italian president Carlo Azeglio Ciampi at the Pope's request and deported to Turkey in 2000.)

"These men may have been sent to promote Pope John XXlll, who passed away on June 3, 1963," Piechota explained of the Sheppton sighting. Piechota was one of numerous researchers attempting to explain what Bova, Fellin and Throne had experienced.

Divine Sighting

Attempting to unravel the mystery of Sheppton, former *Standard Speaker* reporter Ed Conrad interviewed both miners. Each related to Conrad what they had seen. They said, "The Pope was grinning, his arms folded in front of him and appearing to be about half his age he was when he died on June 3."

Says Conrad of the divine sighting, "David Fellin told me perhaps a hundred times that, after Pope John XXIII appeared to both of them at the same time and they briefly discussed his appearance. He never mentioned another word about the Pope to Throne for the duration of their entombment. Fellin explained that, since Throne wasn't religious and didn't know the Pope (or that he had died about two months before), he thought it best not to bring any more attention to their visitor.

"If Hank knew the 'stranger' was dead, he might've gone berserk," Fellin told me. "If he did, it might've been the death of the both of us. I couldn't have survived without Hank and, likewise, Hank wouldn't have been able to survive without me. We needed each other.

"Not another word was made of Pope John XXIII's presence during the remainder of their entombment, even when he was a few short feet away while they were greasing each other before being pulled to the surface," Conrad stated. Conrad described the sighting of the Pope as something of "fact" and "definitely not fiction or faith."

Throne was not a religious person, but after sighting John ("some guy in funny clothes") he appeared to undergo a spiritual conversion. Throne recognized John's picture while hospitalized at Hazleton General. He immediately recognized the picture of "The Pope of Peace" that was hanging on the wall of their hospital room. Throne shouted to his buddy, "That's the guy who was with us Davey," referring to the smiling pope.

Throne was young, troubled, complex. He tended bar after the rescue and became somewhat of a local celebrity. Incredibly, he went back into the mines (somewhere around Nanticoke) and then worked on a bridge building crew. Throne was among the founders of Hazleton's Living Savior Church.

Conrad would play a greater role in the Sheppton incident and personally arranged a special sworn statement titled "Miraculous Coal-Mine Rescue." The document contained the following text, which supported Fellin's sighting of the Pope:

David Fellin signs an affidavit that Pope John Paul XXlll, who died two months before the cave-in, appeared to him and Hank Throne and remained with them until they were rescued 14 days after being entombed.

Upon his rescue it became apparent that Fellin's survival was based upon something profound, some special belief that he clung to during his darkest hour. Fellin's personal physician, Dr. Anthony Fidulla, described his patient as "a spiritual man" and went on to say, "he thinks it was a prime factor in coming through." Anna Fellin maintained that her husband practices his Roman Catholic faith and believes in the Holy Spirit, although she noted that, "Sometimes he misses Sunday Mass because he's very tired."

David Fellin seemed to have figured it out all by himself. While he was entombed, Fellin told Rev. Roman and the rescue team, "I am praying." And he emphasized, "If you don't believe in God down here, you won't believe in Him anywhere."

Their plight either made complete sense or was as random as a crapshoot at Dado's Cafe. And, having survived this horror, whether by luck or providence, in the end, could they ever comprehend the answer to any of this?

Fellin knew that in Christianity, the concept of faith is key. And so, too, is acceptance of God's Mystery, His Awe. He had always known the truth but the horror of Sheppton became the test. It determined the extent of his faith. At some point, the answer unfolded in front of unseeing eyes. His entombment validated what he believed for so many years. That realization filled him with something he had never felt before. Upon being rescued, Fellin confessed, "If you don't believe in God, go through a thing like this. Then you'll know there's a God."

Chapter 15
THE TECHNOLOGY

The Sheppton tragedy was a page torn from the dark past. Due to advanced technological innovations such as Global Position Systems (GPS), Sheppton could not happen today.

With the use of GPS, the location of the miners would have been determined almost immediately. Their rescue would have been initiated without delay. However, in 1963, the rescue team was hampered by outdated maps that provided inaccurate details of mine gangways, knuckles and potential escape routes. Many hours were spent drilling boreholes in the general direction of the trapped men. And in this case of ensuing life and death, coming close was simply not good enough. Fellin and Throne were fortunate that their lives had been spared. But not Louis Bova.

There were a significant number of innovations that played a part in the successful rescue effort and showcased the latest in 1963's technology.

_____ Certainly, the importance of the 50R Bucyrus-Erie high-speed drill cannot be emphasized enough. This beast was capable of drilling through solid rock stratum in a steady and consistent assault.

In The Bucyrus Legacy, the famed corporation provided a brief history of innovative products, including the 50R drill:

In 1952, Bucyrus introduced the 50R, the first commercially accepted large diameter rotary blasthole drill used in the mining industry.

The 50R achieved national fame in 1963 when it was instrumental in rescuing two trapped coal miners in the underground Sheppton Mine at Hazleton, PA. (Note: Actually, the Fellin Mine was located in Sheppton, PA.) This machine, normally used to drill 12-1/4inch holes 100 feet deep, produced a 330 foot, 18 inch diameter rescue hole

_____ The actual drill bit that was to be used in the Bucyrus-Erie 50R was not available in any of the mining projects in the regions encompassing Northeastern Pennsylvania. All of the drill bits were much smaller in size and of little use for the rescue operation. The drill bits were eventually located in Houston, Texas at the Hughes Tool Company. These bits, Tungsten Carbide cutters, were then flown in via the U.S. Navy.

_____ The attempt to use radioactive cobalt to locate the miners was worthy of consideration. It was on the 10th day of entombment that officials of Bloomsburg's U.S. Radium Corporation, including Plant General Manager

W.E. Umstead attempted to pinpoint the exact location of the trapped miners by using a Geiger counter and a particle of radioactive cobalt. The capsule of cobalt, about the size of a pea, contained 400 micro centimeters of cobalt.

Fellin was instructed in the operation of the Geiger counter that had been dropped down to him, but unfortunately, the borehole's location was too far from the point where the Geiger counter would have been able to pick up the radioactive signal. Afterwards, the Atomic Age rescue attempt was deemed to be "furtive but encouraging."

_____ A specially-designed $3,000 camera, operated by technician Elwood Tito and made by the General Precision Corporation of Pleasantville, N.Y., was dropped into the 12-inch borehole. The tiny camera was not equipped for sound but did transmit visual images of the men on a television screen. The camera gave the rescue team a look at the trapped miners for the first time. Throne and Fellin were warned to turn their backs on the camera to avoid being blinded by the sudden glare of the harsh lights.

_____ The U.S. Navy set up a command center at the Sheppton site with a direct line to the Pentagon, in the event that additional equipment or personnel would be needed. U.S. Navy communications experts Lieutenant Harry Potch and Chief Petty officer Richard Young also installed microphones, loudspeakers and a mobile radar station at the location. The U.S. Navy would later fly in the Tungsten carbide drill bits that would eventually rescue the miners.

_____ A seven-and-a-half-foot long cylinder was designed at Hazleton's Pagnotti Enterprises to transport the trapped miners to freedom. The custom-designed steel capsule was nearly as wide as the 18-inch escape hole. This project was abandoned after a bend in the escape hole was discovered. Engineers feared that the capsule could become stuck, trapping the men for a second time.

_____ Phil Margush, radio engineer for Shenandoah's WMBT, snaked down a sensitive microphone, attached to a Voice of Music tape recorder, to amplify any sounds detected. It was to be used to locate the miners, or more specifically, to determine if they were actually alive. After making contact with Throne and Fellin, additional boreholes were drilled in an attempt to locate Louis Bova. Microphones were also used and rescuers yelled down to him but were not able to locate the missing miner.

_____ A revolutionary method of utilizing the energy from coal was being considered during the time of the Sheppton mine disaster. In an attempt to revive the sagging mine industry, the Department of Mines and Mineral Industries introduced an initiative to pioneer state research in the field of liquefaction – the conversion of coal into gasoline and liquid fuel.

In response, the 1963 Pennsylvania Legislature cleared the way for this new research effort and broadened the scope of the seven-year-old Coal Research Board by appropriating $75,000 for the project. The U.S. Office of Coal Research in the Department of the Interior, had already appropriated $440,000 for a nationwide study to determine if such a conversion was technically sound and economically feasible.

_____ Speaking of the unique rescue attempt, author Ronnie Sando said, "We were the first to drill a slant bore hole and retrieve trapped miners buried alive over 300 feet. Everytime I hear that process is being used anywhere in the world, it takes my memory back to the rescue at Sheppton."

It is believed that the Sheppton operation was the first time a borehole was ever drilled and trapped miners pulled to safety using that method. It had never been tried before. Sheppton set precedence for rescues to follow. But what other options were there? The shaft was blocked. It would have been impossible to try to open it due to the timbers that clogged the shaft and the possibility of more deadly cave-ins.

Sando argued that the 1963 rescue "set precedence" for mine rescues to follow and as recent as the 2007 rescue operation at the Murray mine in Huntington, Utah.

According to Hazleton's *Standard Speaker* Reporter Kent Jackson, lessons learned from the Sheppton saga may have saved future lives. He wrote, "The technology developed at Sheppton and refined since then saved nine miners trapped for four days when a cascade of water blocked their escape from the Quecreek Mine in Lincoln County, Somerset County (Pennsylvania) on July 24, 2002.

"Again in 2010, in San Jose, Chile, rescuers followed the Sheppton strategy to lift 33 miners to safety after keeping them alive while they were 2,300 feet below ground for 68 days," Jackson reported.

_____*Life Magazine* photographer George Harvan described the media frenzy that converged upon Sheppton: "The Sheppton disaster was probably the most photographed and watched disaster in the anthracite region. I mean, due to the fact that television was just coming into its own, and the networks were covering it as a big news event. It was covered by each network and local T.V. station in the East. The foreign press was also there."

Harvan's assessment was accurate. There were more than 200 news reporters who camped outside the military-like parameters of the cave-in. CBS sent two television units to the disaster site and Walter Cronkite was expected to broadcast from the Sheppton location. NBC television and radio correspondent Robert Goralski, who came in from New York, was there. Philadelphia's top-rated news anchor John Facenda, of WCAU-TV the CBS television affiliate and "The Voice of God" for NFL Films was also there to file stories of the rescue attempt. The disaster generated international attention. Camera crews and reporters came from England, Japan and Germany to document the rescue attempt.

_____The *Associated Press*, in retrospect, called the Sheppton event the ninth most important international news story of 1963.

And it was *Time Magazine* that observed, "To the townsfolk, Fellin and Throne were heroes. Indeed, to men everywhere, their indomitable will to survive was the stuff of which legends are made."

Chapter 16
EPILOGUE

Sheppton was an anarchist's time bomb.

It had been tick --- tick --- ticking, for a long time.

It exploded on a cool autumn morning, just after 8:00 a.m. A horrible sonic blast, followed by chunks of rock and coal, were baroquely strewn in a random crapshoot. Huge beams, weathered and crisscrossed with coal scars, looked like hieroglyphics and relegated the timber to satanic art. Cruel spikes of coal raked across soft tissue. Lungs burned. Seeing was no longer relevant. There was an odd stillness, and, within microseconds, the stench of death arrived.

The Coal Region has borne witness to countless disasters. So often, days and weeks and months were measured in funerals and chants of the Requiem Mass for the Dead. It happened everywhere. Avondale, Baltimore Tunnel No. 2, City, Knox, Mammouth, Nanticoke No. 1., Twin,

Jeansville, Quecreek, West End and Sheppton, all listed in that ill-fated chronicle of death.

Although the Knox and Jeansville catastrophes claimed more lives, the fourteen-day event in Schuylkill County has captivated and resonated on sundry spiritual and metaphysical levels. Sheppton has always been different, has eerily resounded louder. Sheppton has been pronounced a "continuous, collective hallucination," an out-of-body experience, a miracle by Pope John XXIII, and proof of life after death. *Fate Magazine* described Sheppton as "unmatched in the annals of psychic research." *The Associated Press* called it one of the top news stories of the year.

―――

A tombstone has been erected as a final tribute to Louis J. Bova. The memorial is an easy five-minute walk from Sheppton's Schoolhouse Road, past a rusting Kamatsu earthmover guarding the entrance like a yellow dinosaur. Tall grasses and tall trees protect the hard-to-find gravesite. People leave pennies, and other tributes on top of his stone: a bullet, a VFW button, a beer cap. The tribute is located at the shaft entranceway of the former Fellin Coal Company, and situated above the now-filled-in boreholes. The monument is surrounded on three sides by a plain white picket fence. White stone covers the plot like a blanket. The Sheppton American Legion Post 616 maintains the gravesite, and holds a Memorial Day ceremony there each year.

John Bova, son of Louis, holds the deed to the land. Among the remaining items in his possession include the only photograph of his father --- a photo of his parents on their wedding day. There is also a pocket Bible, a Social Security card and various newspaper clippings. Only those few items and the memories that John Bova has created. He wears a tattoo that reads, "Never Seen, Never forgotten," a tribal marking connecting him to his father. He has also written a song, "Entombed," about the Sheppton ordeal.

Bova has strong beliefs about the mine disaster. He blames Fellin for the cave in that took his father's life. "They were robbing pillars and it was wrong," Bova said. "Nobody wants to say that they were robbing the pillars, but they were. That's why it collapsed. They robbed the pillars and worked their way out of the mine. It's all hushed up. It's all about the money," he said. "Sheppton was a miracle, but it was also a tragedy too. They didn't get my father out. They never got his body."

A stark tomb, 300 feet underneath tons of dirt, rock and coal, is protector of Sheppton's secret. It is the last remaining memorial to one of this century's most baffling mysteries. Preserved by a constant temperature and in total darkness, it protects the answer many have searched for, one that will never be revealed.

In *The Marriage of Heaven and Hell*, William Blake observed, "If the doors of perception were cleansed every thing would appear to man as it is, infinite." In describing his experience with the hallucinogen mescaline, Aldous Huxley expounded upon that theme, "There are things known and there are things unknown, and in between are the doors of perception."

The implications of Blake and Huxley are persuasive. There are events in this world that cannot be explained by rational science, things neither guided by natural law nor verifiable through empirical testing. Sheppton is an anomaly containing only the thinnest rind of scientific veracity. Although interesting and fascinating, Sheppton is a house of cards lacking scientific explanation and empirical proof.

Sheppton is a crazy Rubix Cube with unequal parts of the miraculous, the supernatural and the incomprehensible. "Nothing is so firmly believed as that which is least known," Montaigne asserts. Many believe a miracle occurred in Sheppton. We want to believe. We need to believe. Determined to find an answer, we replace science with faith and arrive at a personal, intimate conclusion. Still, we argue, "Are scientific rules adaptable enough to allow consideration of supernatural forces?" "And, too, is it possible to comprehend elements that lie outside our realm of understanding and empirical knowledge?"

Sheppton exists in a place we are unable to understand. Stuck between darkness and light, it lies between the natural order and the supernatural. In the archives of mining disasters, Sheppton endures as a testament to human suffering and survival, as an acknowledgment of man's inability to comprehend that which is incomprehensible. The Sheppton Mythology, greater than the sum of its parts, will forever remain one of our greatest modern-day mysteries.

Chapter 17
THE TIMELINE

1831 –Black lung disease first described by a doctor in Edinburgh, Scotland, nearly two centuries ago. After performing an autopsy on a coal miner, his lungs revealed shreds of "black carbonaceous colour." The doctor concluded that the illness derived from "the habitual inhalation of a quantity of coal dust with which the atmosphere of a coal-mine must be constantly charged."

September 6, 1869 – Avondale Mining Disaster. Mine fire claimed the lives of 108 miners and two men attempting their rescue at Avondale, PA, located in Plymouth Township.

November 25, 1881 - Angelo Roncalli, who would be elected as Pope John XXIII, was born into a sharecropper family near Bergamo, in the foothills of the Alps.

October 8, 1907 – American writer and author Richard Sharpe Shaver born in Berwick, PA. His "The Shaver Mystery" was published in *Amazing Stories* in 1947. Promoted the "Hollow Earth Theory" to curious readers.

May 9, 1926 – Richard Byrd attempts to be the first to fly to the North Pole. With pilot Floyd Bennett, they fly a Fokker tri-motor airplane about 16 hours. Byrd presented with Medal of Honor.

October 13, 1930: The Miracle at Fatima or The Miracle of the Sun was officially accepted as a miracle by the Roman Catholic Church.

February 19, 1947 - Admiral Richard B. Byrd's secret journal, *The Inner Earth - My Secret Diary*, claimed knowledge of an unknown civilization with technologically advanced inhabitants. Unable to be authenticated the diary is believed to be a hoax.

1948 – Peter Bova, brother of Louis, spent seven days and seven nights trapped in a mine. "Every minute seemed like a day," he said.

1952 - The Federal Coal Mine Safety Act of 1952 provided for annual inspections in certain underground coalmines. Gave the Bureau limited enforcement authority, including power to issue violation notices and imminent danger withdrawal orders. Authorized the assessment of civil penalties against mine operators for noncompliance or for refusing to give inspectors access to mine property.

October 28, 1958 – John XXIII elected Pope at age 77. Headed the Roman Catholic Church for a brief five-year reign.

December 25, 1958 – Pope John XXIII visited prisoners at Rome's Regina Coeli Prison on Christmas Day, his first Christmas as Pope.

May 15, 1961 – Pope John XXIII's first social encyclical, *Mater et Magister* (Mother and Teacher) appeared. He endorsed, to an unprecedented degree, state intervention in socio- political matters but also a wider range of individual and people's rights. Writing on the topic of "Christianity and Social Progress, it taught that the state must sometimes intervene in matters of health care, education, and housing.

June 3, 1963 - John XXIII's second social encyclical, *Pacem in Terris*, appeared shortly before his death. *Pacem in Terris* maintained that peace could only be reached by collaboration between all people of upright conscience, which meant even those involved in movements inspired by erroneous ideologies.

June 3, 1963- Pope John XXlll passes away in hospital in Rome, Italy.

August 13, 1963 - At 7:30 a.m. Dave Fellin arrives "in the hole" and ready for work. By 8:00 a.m., along with Louis Bova and Henry Throne, they fill their first buggy with coal and sent it to the top. As the buggy begins the return trip, the cave in occurs.

August 14, 1963 – A rescue attempt is impossible. Emergency rescue workers are unable to enter the slope due to continued cave-ins and deadly black damp gas.

_____ Emergency fans are used to help ventilate and draw off the deadly gasses in the slope.

August 15, 1963 - Cave-ins continue for days and hamper any possible rescue attempts.

_____ Requests were made for both federal and state funding to pay for the rescue operations. Total cost requested was estimated around $60,000.

_____ Officials develop plan to fill present shaft and then dig an alternate one. Project was estimated to take fifty-days to complete and was soon scratched.

August 16, 1963 - Relatives of the trapped miners encourage United Mine Worker's organization in Hazleton to intervene in the situation.

_____ W.A. "Tony" Boyle, President of the UMWA, assigned Lewis Evans, former Secretary of Mines and Mineral Industries, to investigate Sheppton accident and to render whatever assistance he could.

August 17, 1963 - John Labuda, the original developer of the mine slope prior to the Fellin Coal Company taking it over, provides technical information on depth of the slope from the knuckle and east gangway.

_____ Pittsburgh's William Glunt Drilling Company is contacted and agree to provide use of their Davey 6-inch rotary drill and expert personnel. The equipment is located in Export, PA, nearly 250-miles away.

_____ The Davey 6-inch drilling equipment did not arrive at the scene until around 1:30 p.m.

_____ Sprague and Henwood Rota-drilling equipment arrives from Scranton, PA. around 4:00 p.m.

_____ At 6:30 p.m. the 6-inch-wide drill begins to penetrate through 331 feet of rock in an attempt to locate the trapped miners.

August 18, 1963 - Around 11:00 p.m. the 6-inch-wide drill breaks through the chamber and makes contact with Fellin and Throne. There is no sign of Bova.

_____ A light and microphone are lowered through the borehole to the entombed miners.

_____ John Biros voice contact is established with Fellin and Throne shortly before midnight.

August 19, 1963 - Rescuers began drilling a separate borehole in the direction where Bova was believed to be located. The drilling operation was stopped after the six-inch-wide lifeline hole drifted.

August 20, 1963 - Drilling of the first escape hole was called off around the 193-foot depth when Throne and Fellin reported that the ceiling was cracking and they feared another cave-in.

August 21, 1963 - In an attempt to reach Fellin and Throne, a second twelve-inch escape hole is started around 7:00 a.m. By midafternoon the drill had reached a depth of 162 feet through solid rock.

_____ Rescue attempts are delayed for six hours after a broken drive shaft stops the drilling operation and the giant 65-ton rig.

_____ Fellin and Throne report that they have re-established verbal contact with Louis Bova after some 40-hours. Bova remained separated from them by a pile of debris in the tunnel.

August 22, 1963 - Governor William Scranton visits the rescue site offering his support and encouragement.

_____ Officials of U.S. Radium Corporation attempt to pinpoint the exact area where two of the three miners are trapped. They utilized a Geiger counter and a capsule containing 400 micro centimeters of cobalt, about the size of a pea. Their efforts would prove to be unsuccessful.

August 23, 1963 - drills through the rooftop of the mine chamber with a twelve-inch wide borehole.

_____ A special $3000 camera, operated by technician Elwood Tito and made by the General Precision Corporation of Pleasantville, N.Y. is dropped down the 12-inch borehole. Rescuers are able to see Throne and Fellin on a television screen.

August 24, 1963 - Pennsylvania State Police barricaded all roads in the area surrounding the Oneida slope. Police were fearful that sightseers would hamper efforts to rescue the three miners. Only authorized persons are being allowed into the area.

_____ W.A. "Tony" Boyle, president of the United Mine Workers, visited the rescue scene. A brief shoving match occurred between members of the UMW and Independent Miners Association. Fellin and Throne are both members of the rival IMA.

August 25, 1963 - Three of Louis Bova's brothers visit the rescue site. Tony, John and Dan, who believe that their brother is still alive, were critical of rescuers whom, they believed, were taking too long to drill exploratory probes to find the missing miner.

_____ Fellin and Throne celebrated their last night entombed by having a special Sunday night dinner party. Throne requested fig bars, graham crackers and sourball hard candy while Fellin asked for hot peppers and bologna.

August 27, 1963 - Rescue crews bore through the debris to open a 17 ½-inch hole – wide enough to hoist the miners to safety. The borehole was completed at 6:25.

_____ At 2:07 a.m. Henry Throne is lifted to safety. His passage through the borehole took fifteen-minutes.

_____ David Fellin is hoisted from the shaft at 2:41

_____ Dr. Anthony Fidulla reports that David Fellin has promised his wife Anna that he is giving up mining.

August 28, 1963 - Rescue experts tried unsuccessfully for two ½ hours to make contact with entombed miner Louis Bova. H.B. Chambury, Pennsylvania secretary of mines told a news conference "we are not even thinking of stopping."

August 29, 1963 - A sensitive microphone on an intercom system is lowered more than 300 feet into the chamber where Louis Bova is believed to be trapped. For hours the rescuers shout "Lou! Lou! Hello there, Lou!"

August 29, 1963 – David Fellin's 'affidavit" printed in the *Philadelphia Inquirer*. He said, "My mind was clear down there in the mine. It's still clear."

August 30, 1963-

_____ The Associated Press lists the Sheppton mining disaster as the 9th most significant news story of 1963.

September 7, 1963 - The Pennsylvania Department of Mines and Mineral Industries petitioned the Schuylkill

County Court to issue an order closing the mine or to order Bova's body recovered.

November 10, 1965- Because of the Sheppton event, "The Anthracite Coal Mining Laws of Pennsylvania for Underground Mines, Act 346" was revised to delete the exemption that small mines had previously enjoyed.

September 16, 1966 – Calling the Federal Metal and Nonmetallic Mine Safety Act of 1966 "a most historic and humane piece of legislation," President Lyndon B. Johnson remarked, "Beyond saving the lives and the limbs of many men who labor under the earth, this act will enable wives to rest a little easier when their husbands leave home for work each morning. And it will enable many children to grow to adulthood with their fathers still living and still earning a livelihood for the entire family."

December 30, 1969 - The Coal Act (Federal Coal Mine Health and Safety Act of 1969) was more stringent than any previous Federal mining legislation. Included surface as well as underground coalmines, required two annual inspections of every surface coal mine and four at every underground coal mine. Provided compensation for miners who were totally and permanently disabled by black lung.

December 30, 1969 - The Federal Coal Mine Health and Safety Act of 1969, generally referred to as the Coal Act, was more comprehensive than any previous Federal mining legislation. The Coal Act included surface as well as underground coalmines; required two annual inspections of every surface coal mine and four at every underground coal mine, and dramatically increased federal enforcement powers in coalmines. Required monetary penalties for all violations, and established criminal penalties for knowing and willful violations. The safety standards for all coalmines were strengthened, and health standards were adopted. Provided compensation for miners who were totally and permanently disabled by the respiratory disease pneumoconiosis or "black lung".

December 31, 1969- Joseph A. Yablonski and his wife Margaret and daughter Charlotte are found murdered in their beds in Clarksville, PA. W.A. "Tony" Boyle, President of the UMWA, found guilty.

April 1974 – William Anthony "Tony" Boyle sentenced to three consecutive terms of life in prison.

January 28, 1977 – William Anthony "Tony" Boyle three consecutive terms of life in prison overturned. Resentenced to three consecutive terms of life in prison in February 1978. Died in prison in 1985.

March 1, 1977 – Nine miners were drowned to death at the Porter Tunnel Mine in Tower City, PA., after their mine chamber flooded.

August 10, 1985 – David Fellin undergoes a polygraph test to ascertain if he was truthful about his supernatural experiences in the mine. No reactions indicative of deception were recorded during the test.

May 31, 1985 - William Anthony "Tony" Boyle dies in prison. Boyle had been sentenced to three consecutive terms of life in prison for the deaths of union leader Joseph A. Yablonski and his family.

June 1, 1987 – Elisabeth Kubler-Ross, in response to Ed Conrad's manuscript "Look For The Light," writes letter acknowledging Fellin and Thrones' out-of-body trips. Affirms that life continues even after the physical body dies.

March 29,1990 – David Fellin lived for 27-more years after his Sheppton rescue. He died two weeks before his 85th birthday.

May 1998 – Hank Throne lived 35-more years following his rescue. He died at age 63.

July 28, 2002 - The bore hole technology developed at Sheppton saved nine miners trapped for 77 hours when a cascade of water blocked their escape from the Quecreek Mine in western Pennsylvania.

March, 2004 – James A. Goodwin publishes *Two Weeks Under: The Sheppton Mine Disaster/ Miracle* (Coal Hole Productions).

June 26, 2005 – Adventurer Steve Curry organizes expedition to go to the North Pole in search of polar openings. Curry charters a nuclear icebreaker with the capacity for 108 passengers for the purpose of taking a group to the interior of the earth.

July 16, 2007 – J. *Ronnie Sando publishes The Famous Sheppton Mine Rescue: The Untold Story: The Blood and Sweat of the Rescue Team* (Publish America).

July 5, 2013 – Reigning Pope Francis declared John XXIII a Saint based on his merits of opening the Second Vatican Council.

August 14, 2013 - A ceremony marking the 50th anniversary of the Sheppton Mine Disaster took place at the grave of Louis Bova. Most Rev. John O. Barres, bishop of Allentown, conducted the Mass held at St. Joseph Roman Catholic Church, with about 200 people attending.

2013 –Coal Worker's pneumoconiosis resulted in 25,000 global deaths in 2013, down from 29,000 deaths in 1990, according to Lancet.

April 27, 2014 Pope John XXIII canonized in St. Peter's Square, alongside Pope John Paul II.

August 22, 2015- A state historical marker commerating the Sheppton Mine Disaster and rescue is unveiled. Marker states that the "borehole technique was used for mine rescues worldwide, notably Quecreek (2002) and Chile (2010)."

November 13, 2015: The motion picture, "The 33" is released. Film depicts the 2010 Chilean mining disaster that entombed 33 miners in 100 degree temperatures for more than two months. The borehole technique, first utilized at Sheppton, was used to rescue the miners, however there is no mention of Sheppton in the film.

REFERENCES

Altoonians Son Acclaimed Hero At Cave in Site. (1963). *Altoona Mirror*. Retrieved at http://www.eastuniontownship.com/index.php?option=com_content&view=article&id=87&Itemid=94

Bova, Peter. Interview. *Pottstown Mercury*. Date unknown.

Bucyrus International Inc. *RitchieWiki*. Retrieved from http://www.ritchiewiki.com/wiki/index.php/Bucyrus

Budd, D. (2013). Trapped Miners Meet the Paranormal. *BellaOnline. The Voice of Women*. Retrieved from http://www.bellaonline.com/ArticlesP/art55544.asp

Bureau of Labor Statistics, U.S. Department of Labor (2010). Career Guide to Industries, 2010-11 Edition. Retrieved at at http://www.bls.gov/oco/cg/cgs004.htm

Caverns, Dungeons and Labyrinths. (Date Unknown). *The Watcher Files*. Retrieved from http://www.thewatcherfiles.com/cosmicconflict/caverns.htm

Clemente-Arnaldo, N.V. (2009). Pope John XXIII: The Good Pope. *Totus Tuus Maria*. Retrieved from http://www.all-about-the-virgin-mary.com/pope-john-xxiii.html

Conrad, E. (1990). The Second Greatest Story Ever Told. Retrieved from http://www.edconrad.org/lifeafterdeath/page2_files/body.html

Conrad, E. (2007). A 6-inch borehole – the first such attempt in a mining rescue attempt anywhere in the world. *Standard Speaker*. Retrieved from http://www.eastuniontownship.com/index.php?option=com_content&view=article&id=95&Itemid=98

Construction Begins on $1.7 Million Luzerne County Mine Reclamation Project: Cranberry West Site to be Made Safe, Readied for Potential Economic Development. (2010). Retrieved from http://www.portal.state.pa.us/portal/server.pt/community/news_releases/14288

Duffy, J.P.*Target America: Hitler's Plan to Attack the United States*. Guilford, CT.: The Lyons Press. 2006

Goodman, J.A. *Two Weeks Under: The Sheppton Mine Disaster/Miracle*. Bloomsburg, PA: Coal Hole Productions.2003.

Haddock, K. (2005) Churn Drills Bored Early holes. *Construction Equipment*. Retrieved from http://www.constructionequipment.com/article/CA6280170.html

History of Mine Safety and Health Legislation. (2015). *United States Department of Labor*. Retrieved from http://www.msha.gov/MSHAINFO/MSHAINF2.HTM

Hollow Earth Hypothesis (2012). Retrieved from http://www.crystalinks.com/agartha.html

Holzer, H. *Ghosts: True Encounters with the World Beyond*. New York: Black Dog & Leventhal Publishers, Inc. 1997.

Ivory, K. *Pennsylvania Disasters: True Stories of Tragedy and Survival.* Guilford, CT: Insider's Guide. 2007.

Jackson, K. (August 15, 2013). Rescue techniques saved lives decades later. *Standard Speaker.*

Knox Mine Disaster. Retrieved from http://explorepahistory.com/hmarker.php?markerId=398

Kraus, W. (August 25, 1988). Mine Disaster Was 25 Years Ago Sheppton Cave-In Claimed One Life. *The Morning Call.*

Kubiszewski, I. (September 4, 2008). Federal Coal Mine Safety Act of 1952, United States. *The Encyclopedia of Earth.* Retrieved from http://www.eoearth.org/view/article/152741/

O'Boyle, B. (2007). Book salutes 1963 rescue. *Times Leader.*

Lunn, A. (2011). Exploring the Myth of the Men in Black. *UFO Evidence.* Retrieved from http://www.ufoevidence.org/documents/doc1691.htm

McAuliffe, J. (2007). Reflections of Poe. *The Times Tribune.* Retrieved from http://www.glassprismband.com/tribune.pdf

McGee, R. (March 9, 2014). *United States Mine Rescue Association.* Personal Communications.

McKerns, G.L. *The Black Rock That Built America: A Tribute to the Anthracite Coal Miners.* Bloomington, IN.: Xlibris Corporation. 2007.

Mine Accidents and Disasters. (2010). Porter Tunnel Mine: Kocher Coal Company. *United States Mine Rescue*

Association. Retrieved from http://www.usmra.com/saxsewell/portertunnel.htm

Miner's Son, Miner's Photographer: The Life and Work of George Harvan (2000). *The Journal of MultiMedia History*. Retrieved from http://www.albany.edu/jmmh/vol3/harvan/interview/harv4.htm

Monitz, K. (August 13, 2013). Lost miner's son never escaped Sheppton, either. *Standard Speaker*.

Monitz, K. (August 15, 2013). Locals recall Sheppton's story. *Standard Speaker*.

Monteiro, G. (1964). Oak Mine Timbers. *Western Folklore*. Retrieved from http://www.jstor.org/pss/1498269

Murley, C. (2005). Knox Mine Disaster. *Underground Mines*. Retrieved from http://www.undergroundminers.com/knox.html

Nadeau, B.L. (April 26, 2014). Popes, Saints, Miracles, Weird Relics and Odd Omens Converge on Rome. *The Daily Beast*. Retrieved from http://www.thedailybeast.com/articles/2014/04/26/popes-saints-miracles-weird-relics-and-odd-omens-converge-on-rome.html

Ney, F. (2003). Sheppton Mine Disaster: 40 Years Later. *News Item*.

Norman, E. *The Under-People*. New York: Award Books. 1969.

O'Boyle, B. (2007). Book salutes 1963 rescue. *Times Leader*.

O'Grady, D. (November 1996). Almost A Saint: Pope John XXIII. *St. Anthony Messenger*. Retrieved from http://www.americancatholic.org/Messenger/Nov1996/feature1.asp

Pennsylvania: Start of a Legend? (1963). *Time*. Retrieved at http://www.time.com/time/magazine/article/0,9171,870450,00.html

Petroff, D., Windfield, N. (April 28, 2014). Vatican sees historic day of four popes. Associated Press.

Piechota, M. (2005). Religion and Ufology. *IRAAP Messenger*.

Ragan, T. (August 15, 2013). Authors recount famous two weeks. *Standard Speaker*.

Reed, J. (May 9, 2014). Great Gift of New Saints Reminds Us of Our Call to Holiness, Bishop Says as Diocese Celebrates Canonizations. *The Catholic Witness*.

Sando, J.R. *The Famous Sheppton Mine Rescue: The Untold Story: The Blood and Sweat of the Rescue Team*. Frederick, MD PublishAmerica. 2006.

Schmeer, B. (March, 1965). The Entombed Miners' Staircase to Heaven. *Fate*, 28-37.

Sheppton Mine Disaster 50 Years Later. (August 14, 2013). *WYLN Topic A*.

Stoppler, M. (2010). Endorphins: Natural Pain and Stress Fighters. *MedicineNet.com*. Retrieved from http://www.medicinenet.com/script/main/art.asp?articlekey=55001

The Bucyrus Legacy. (2005). Retrieved from http://www.bucyrus.com/media/24488/history%20brochure%200105.pdf

Throne, H. (1963) Throne's Account: Throne Tells How He and Fellin Survived Entombment. *Pottsville Republican*. Retrieved from http://www.eastuniontownship.com/index.php?option=com_content&view=article&id=84&Itemid=95

Wagner, V. (2004). R & R Coal. *Vanwagnermusic.com*. Retrieved from http://www.vanwagnermusic.com/coal.html

Wallace, P.A.W. (1970). *Indians in Pennsylvania*. Pennsylvania Historical and Museum Commission.

Waller, M. (1998) Sheppton Folks Recall Mine Disaster: Throne's death finds Sheppton folks recall mine disaster vividly. Rescue put patch in international spotlight. Pottsville *Evening Herald*.

ABOUT THE AUTHOR

Maxim W. Furek is the former Publisher of *Timothy*, a tabloid magazine supporting Pennsylvania musical talent. He is the unofficial biographer of the Jordan Brothers and has been instrumental in promoting their legacy. In 2011 Furek inducted the group into the Schuylkill Arts Hall of Fame. He has written over 100 articles on music and has contributed liner notes for the Glass Prism, Hybrid Ice and others. His column, "Cultural Trends," appears in *Counselor, the Magazine for Addiction and Behavioral Professionals*. A forthcoming book, *Celebrity Blood Voyeurism*, is a work-in-progress.

Also by the author…

The Death Proclamation of Generation X: A Self-Fulfilling Prophesy of Goth, Grunge and Heroin. New York: i-Universe. 2008.

The Jordan Brothers: A Musical Biography of Rock's Fortunate Sons. Berwick, PA: Kimberley Press. 1986.

Made in the USA
Charleston, SC
13 August 2016